"KNOWING THE EXPECTATIONS OF THE JOURNEY AHEAD: that well describes Dr. Rob Franzblau's priceless contribution to the requisite library of the music professionals. Rob has successfully looked at this important decision many young people face as they enter their college careers; EVERY aspiring high school to-be music major should study the book, every college freshman should consume the wisdom within the pages, and all who are connected with music learning and music making can garner immeasurable benefits authored by Dr. Franzblau. This is not a book you *should* read, this is a book you *must* read."

— **Dr. Tim Lautzenheiser**, President, Attitude Concepts for Today, Inc.

"The content of this book will be especially useful to post-elementary guidance counselors seeking to provide support for students contemplating a career in music education, as well as their parents."

— **Jon Becker**, Arts & Education Consultant (former music faculty for Oconomowoc WI public schools and music education department chair for Westminster Choir College, Princeton NJ)

"I liked how he addressed chapters to different groups (parents, kids, counselors, teachers). It drew me into reading chapters not related to my group (parents), to understand what the other groups might be thinking or wanting to know. He was concise, logical, and provided a wealth of information without being boring. As you can see, it was a quick and easy read."

— **Vicki Feltman**, Music Parent, Homestead High School, Cupertino, CA

"Franzblau's new book is filled with advice and helpful information that will help a prospective music student prepare for their college/university/music school study. School music teachers, guidance counselors and parents should read and refer to the recommendations contained in this book."

— **Frank L. Battisti**, Emeritus Conductor, New England Conservatory Wind Ensemble

"As one who has devoted a 30-year career to the music education profession, and now being a music parent myself, I see the process of educating our young people through an entirely new lens. Not only is this book a great resource to the young people who are contemplating or preparing for a noble profession, it is a MUST-READ for every PARENT. Dr. Franzblau's contribution provides insights we will all benefit from."

— **L. Scott McCormick**, Founder & President AMP — The National Association of Music Parents

"Robert Franzblau provides a thorough and thoughtful book for how and why the high school music student should consider majoring in music. Not only will the student musician enjoy reading this thought-provoking and question-answering book, but so will parents like myself who have been blessed to have children gifted in music. This is a must-read and a welcomed addition to any high school library and music director or counselor's office."

— **Marc C. Whitt**, former president of the Madison Central High School (KY) Band Boosters, 9-year band dad, and National Association of Music Parents AMPassador

"This is a must-read for any parent who has a child considering music as a major in college. As a lifelong music educator and parent of a 17-year-old son who wants to major in music, I can validate everything this book has to offer. Rob has done a masterful job combining his keen insight into the college audition process along with the nuts and bolts information necessary for being totally prepared to enter college. Every high school music educator and counselor should own a copy of this book!

— **Steve Andre**, Director of Fine Arts, Mesquite ISD; Mesquite, Texas,
Past President, Texas Music Educators Association

"Dr. Franzblau has written a unique and most useful book. There is no text in the field useful for multiple audiences. The perception is that music is a specialized field and one can only perform or teach. Selecting a quality college program in music, however, does not narrow one's options. At my institution, graduates have been accepted to graduate school in all fields, including law, business, medicine, and technology. Others have accepted immediate employment due to the social and work skills learned in a quality program. These individuals were not lucky; they followed the guidance proffered by Professor Franzblau in this text."

— **Richard Colwell**, Professor Emeritus, University of Illinois

"While our universities and conservatoriums in Australia work in a very different way to those in the United States, it is equally as true here as it is in the States, that those entering our education institutions for the purpose of gaining a music degree are not being given the wise council they need prior to making their decisions. As a result, wonderful young people are spending precious years pursuing goals that ultimately will lead them nowhere, resulting in frustrations that they could well do without as they try to make headway in an ever increasingly difficult environment.

Your book clearly articulates a path that all parents, councillors and students would be well advised to follow. It clearly states the facts as they really are and lays it on the line in an easy to read, easy to understand, making-lots-of-sense manner."

— **Russell Hammond**, Chairman/Musical Director — the Australian Wind
Orchestra, Honorary member — American Bandmasters Association,
Founding President — The Australian Band and Orchestra Directors Association,
Fellow of the National Band Association Academy of Wind and Percussive Arts

"Rob Franzblau has done an extraordinary thing with this book. With an insight born of experience he explains in detail the role of the Guidance Counselor in the care and feeding of future music educators. I have never read a more complete and succinct description of their specific and vital role. It should occupy a place on the desk of every counselor."

— **Dave Reul,** Past President, American School Band Directors Association

SO YOU WANT TO BE A MUSIC MAJOR

A Guide for High School Students, Their Parents, Guidance Counselors, and Music Teachers

 ROBERT FRANZBLAU

Published by
Meredith Music Publications
a division of G.W. Music, Inc.
1584 Estuary Trail, Delray Beach, Florida 33483
http://www.meredithmusic.com

MEREDITH MUSIC PUBLICATIONS and its stylized double M logo are trademarks of
MEREDITH MUSIC PUBLICATIONS, a division of G.W. Music, Inc.

Cover and text design: Shawn Girsberger

International Standard Book Number: 978-1-57463-378-8
Cataloging-in-Publication Data is on file with the Library of Congress.
Library of Congress Control Number: 2013941519
Printed and bound in U.S.A.

PREFACE

The one hundred-plus websites cited in this book are not supplemental, they are central to its usefulness. Links to all the web pages can all be found, arranged by chapter and page number, at www.ric.edu/faculty/rfranzblau. Readers are encouraged to use this resource.

DEDICATION

To Buz Hoefer, Tim Lautzenheiser, and Frank Battisti, models for what high school and college music education could be.

ACKNOWLEDGEMENTS

I wish to acknowledge, first and always, my wife Shelly for her patience, support, and level head. My father encouraged, critiqued, and proofread this project from start to finish. Dr. Cody Clark provided invaluable perspective as a high school guidance counselor. Dr. Richard Colwell was generous with his time and analytical eye. Colleagues around the country, especially those in the Facebook Band Director Group, offered several excellent suggestions for this work. Dr. Tim Lautzenheiser deserves credit for planting the idea for this book in my brain. Mostly, I want to thank my students, past and present, for helping me learn what students need from their music teacher. You are the reason that we in the music education profession keep teaching.

Contents

Introduction

Not far from where I live, the New England Patriots have established an impressive record: since Bill Belichick was hired as the team's head coach in 2000, they have won three Super Bowls, five AFC Championship Games, and ten AFC East titles, while amassing a record of 168–63. Belichick has earned a reputation as a perfectionist regarding football fundamentals: blocking, tackling, and ball security, to name a few. Whether you love Belichick or hate him, you've got to admire his focus on fundamentals and the results he's achieved.

When anything is pursued seriously, the fundamental knowledge, skills, and attitudes — or as educators would say, basic skills in the cognitive, psychomotor, and affective domains — must be developed first. They establish a solid foundation on which all subsequent learning is built, and they need to be absorbed so deeply and become so instinctive that they can be performed without thinking.

In a similar way, preparing to be a college music major is like preparing for any sport: in both cases, the goal is to learn the fundamentals so well they become automatic. (In many other ways, of course, sports and music are COMPLETELY different!)

This book is written for high school musicians (and their parents, guidance counselors, and teachers) to identify in detail the fundamental knowledge, skills, and attitudes that college music majors need in order to be successful, and to encourage their development in those who aspire towards a career in music. Specific exercises and drills are suggested, along with supporting online resources. It is based on 25 years of experience as a music teacher in elementary through graduate schools, including hearing about 1,000 auditions by prospective college music majors. It is also based on personal conversations, online forums, and survey questions that asked "What entry-level knowledge, skills, and attitudes are needed for success in a college music program?" and "How should students who want to major in music at college be preparing for this in high school?"

Before the "what" and "how" are addressed, however, it is vital to ask "why." Chapter One begins with this most fundamental question: why major in music?

CHAPTER 1 | Why Major in Music?

Personally, I am always ready to learn,
although I do not always like being taught."

— WINSTON CHURCHILL

So you're thinking about majoring in music in college? If you do, you'll have lots of company — each year, more than 90,000 students are enrolled in Bachelor's degree music programs in American colleges, universities, and conservatories.[1] They take classes in music theory, ear training, and music history, they practice their instrument or voice every day and attend weekly private lessons, and they perform in small and large ensembles. The common core of "general education" classes in math, science, history, and literature occupies a significant portion of their classwork, too.

About one-fifth of these students are in pre-professional programs designed to prepare them to teach music, and which culminate in student teaching and certification by their state department of education. Another one-fourth pursue degrees in music performance, where the emphasis is squarely on developing the skills and knowledge needed for a performing career. Roughly two-fifths are admitted to liberal arts programs in music, and another 15% are working

---

1   HEADS Data Summary 2011-2012, National Association of Schools of Music

toward degrees in specialties such as church music, composition, music therapy, music business, recording technology, and music history.[2]

Unfortunately, a relatively low percentage of these students ultimately earn the music degrees they begin. In my position as a college music teacher, every year I see good students, who in many cases are also very good musicians, change their majors or drop out of school entirely, sometimes after pursuing a music degree for years.

Don't misunderstand: everyone needs freedom to find their passion, their mission in life, their major. I don't advocate finishing a degree that you discover isn't what you want, just because that's the major you started. A music degree certainly isn't for everyone. What WOULD be great, however, is to see freshmen music majors have a deeper understanding of what college music study entails, because these students will be less likely to meet with frustration, disappointment, and dissatisfaction in college. One, two, or three years of college music classes — classes that may not count towards your eventual degree — can also be expensive.

My goals for this book are 1) to help guide you toward an informed choice of college major if you're considering music, and 2) to help you enter a college music program more fully prepared for success. Some of you who would have started as music majors may change your minds after reading this book; others may find a deeper commitment to study music. If you do eventually graduate with a music degree, my hope is that you will get more out of college music study by bringing a solid foundation to your freshman year. And I hope those of you who graduate with music education degrees will be able to more deeply inspire your future students because you have gained a more comprehensive music education of your own in college.

2   http://nces.ed.gov/programs/digest/d12/tables/dt12_290.asp

YOU WILL GRADUATE COLLEGE WITH A BACHELOR'S DEGREE. Although it seems to be stating the obvious, earning a degree in music is STILL earning a college degree, the universally accepted "ticket" to success in our society. A recent study estimated that, on average, people with a bachelor's degree earn almost a million dollars more over the course of their careers than those with only a high school diploma. If a bachelor's degree is so valuable, why not spend that effort concentrating on a subject that you're interested in? In all likelihood, you will change jobs several times throughout your working life; for many people, it may make more sense to earn a bachelor's degree in an area which challenges them on a variety of personal levels (which music does), even if they don't eventually settle in a career in that specific field.

IT CAN LEAD TO A FULFILLING CAREER WITH MUSIC. A life of creating beauty and bringing it to others is a good life. It's easy to lose perspective and get consumed with the day-to-day problems and challenges in any career (including music), but what we do as artists is akin to magic. Where else but in the arts do people come together simply to create and share in an emotional experience, with no winners or losers? Where else but in a musical collaboration do people work together so interdependently in order to attain the indefinable? Aesthetic experiences have no material or utilitarian purpose; their aim is to connect us with that which is beyond this world. These experiences have powerful and lasting effects on people, and being part of the process — whether as a composer, performer, or teacher — is both humbling and exalting, and infinitely rewarding.

IT CAN PREPARE YOU FOR A CAREER OR GRADUATE SCHOOL OUTSIDE OF MUSIC. In a 1978 essay[3], Dr. Lewis Thomas suggested that students who major in the humanities fare just as well (if not better) in medical school than those whose undergraduate majors are in the science-heavy "pre-med" area. In 1981, John Bruer and Kenneth

---

3   New England Journal of Medicine; 1978; 298:1180

Warren found that music majors were just as likely to be accepted in medical school as biochemistry majors — and these two led all other majors[4].

At least as much as any college degree, or maybe more, a music degree shows the world that you have talent, intelligence, determination, creativity, and the ability to work with others. These are precisely the traits that employers and graduate schools look for in applicants. A 4.0 grade point average is impressive to a potential employer or graduate school, regardless of major.

IT IS A GREAT WAY TO EXPAND YOUR MIND. The academic study of music is a fascinating way to explore human culture and civilization. The arts do not exist in a vacuum; they are always a product of their time and place. Medieval plainchant and art serve as glimpses into the power of the Roman Catholic Church at that time; Johann Sebastian Bach's music offers the same insights into the influence that the Lutheran church had in German society of the late Baroque. The growing nationalism heard in European music of the late 19th and early 20th centuries was a reflection of an increasingly divisive political mood, which ultimately became manifest in two devastating world wars — which in turn had far-reaching influences on music. Listening to recordings of Billie Holliday can lead to a deeper inquiry into the history of segregation in America. Even theories of subatomic physics like the Heisenberg Uncertainty Principle have their aesthetic parallels in the music of John Cage. As one of the oldest forms of human culture, music connects with knowledge in other fields. In-depth knowledge of music creates a mental framework upon which to arrange learning in almost every other field of human endeavor, and it is an indicator of an educated mind.

Sometimes, however, other issues factor into students' decisions to major in music. Despite the best of intentions, many of these don't hold up under closer inspection. . . .

4   JAMA, 1981; 245(4):364-366

REASONS **NOT** TO MAJOR IN MUSIC:

Not because it will be fun

I once worked with a master teacher in a world-class instrumental music program in a Wisconsin school district. He had a great saying whenever students started complaining about the level of work that he expected from them: "Whoever told you that band was supposed to be fun was lying to you."

The Oxford Dictionary defines "fun" as "amusing, entertaining, or enjoyable." Things that are fun require little or nothing from you, except to just sit back and take it in. Their rewards are immediate and their benefits are short-lived. Disneyland, a great movie, a fantastic first date — these are fun! Although they may be a bit scary, taking you out of your comfort zone, fun things never really demand anything from you beyond the present moment. In fact, part of their whole appeal is their intense connection to the present moment — a feeling of aliveness and "presence" that can be addictive.

A word like "rewarding," on the other hand, implies a whole different level of commitment. It's not about instant gratification any more, but return on investment. What you get out is in direct proportion to what you put in, just like anything else in life. Much deeper than "fun," the feelings you get when you've mastered a difficult passage, collaborated with others in an expressive performance, or uncovered beauty through analysis and active listening are yours forever. This level of satisfaction is available only to those who earn it through sustained effort. Therefore, . . .

Not because it will be easy

If you're serious about your education, there is no such thing as an easy major — every field of knowledge can and should be pursued with depth, intellectual curiosity, and rigor. College professors in every department are thrilled to have hard-working, committed students who want to push beyond the minimum requirements and learn everything they can about their subject.

Frequently, however, high school graduates haven't yet "caught the bug" for a particular field of study, but they know that getting a college degree is important. That's okay; in fact, that's good. Truthfully, many students also go to college to get away from home, grow up, assert their individuality, meet new people, party, or some combination of these. Though they may sense the general direction their career may eventually take, their choice of college major is less important than just "going to college."

Students like these who have yet to pick a major often discuss what the "easy" majors are. Dozens of websites, online forums, and blogs are devoted to this question, which always seemed a bit irrelevant to me. As one webpage states, "There's nothing wrong with wanting to earn a college degree with as little effort as possible. That would allow you more free time and the opportunity to explore what your passions are.[5]" Excuse me? "Exploring your passion" is a great way to actually CHOOSE your major. And of course, right next to the article's title "Easiest College Majors" is a picture of a violinist. Don't believe it.

WHAT'S HARD ABOUT MAJORING IN MUSIC?

TIME MANAGEMENT. Unlike most college majors, musicians are not only learning in the cognitive domain (knowledge about music theory, history, pedagogy, and so on), but significant learning has to take place in the psychomotor domain as well (performance skills on your major instrument, and often secondary instruments). Building these skills takes sustained effort over long periods of time. Malcolm Gladwell and others have cited the "10,000 hour rule," which suggests that it takes that much practice at anything to become an expert.[6] Learning how to prioritize, budget, and manage your time is something no one can teach you, but it's an essential skill. There are only 24 hours in each day; some days you'll be so tired you'll wish there were time to catch a nap.

5 http://www.campusexplorer.com/college-advice-tips/7DF05979/
   Easiest-College-Majors/
6 http://en.wikipedia.org/wiki/Outliers_(book)

MUSIC THEORY AND SIGHT SINGING. These courses, required in every undergraduate music degree during the first two years, separate the men from the boys and the women from the girls. Although professors don't make these courses hard on purpose, intentionally reducing the number of music majors in some evil master plan, they also know theory and sight singing establish the foundation for all future musical understanding; they form the common language all musicians communicate with, regardless of instrument. Unfortunately, most incoming freshman music majors have had little or no training in even the fundamentals of theory or sight singing; their music education has usually been focused solely on developing performance skills. The demands of music theory and sight singing have changed many college music majors into former music majors.

PIANO. Some music degrees, particularly those in music education, require all students to take class piano instruction and often pass a proficiency exam. The requirements can be intimidating — transposing at sight, improvising accompaniments to simple tunes, playing scales and basic chord progressions in all twelve keys, and so on. Just like skills on your major instrument, developing piano skills takes sustained effort over a long period of time.

UNUSUAL HOURS. At 9:00 pm, the halls of a college English or math department are empty. Go into the music building however, and you're likely to see dozens of students taking a break from a rehearsal, others working in the computer lab on music theory homework, and lots of others upstairs in practice rooms. Campus security officers often have to "evict" music majors from the building each night at closing time. It's just a fact of college music life: you may have a dorm room where you sleep, but you'll be living in the music building.

STRESS. Stress often happens when we're put in new environments, and this applies to schooling, too. In most high school courses, you were expected to come up with the "correct" answer ("If two trains leave the same station travelling in opposite directions...."). In music, however, multiple solutions to a problem are frequently valued ("Very nice — now play that same phrase again, but emphasize the

F#, not the G"). Students who are flexible in their learning styles are often less stressed, happier, and more successful music majors.

PUBLIC PERFORMANCE. If the thought of having every performance evaluated by friends, teachers, and total strangers makes you nervous, don't worry. That's absolutely normal. Most music majors (and most professionals) get nervous to some extent. On the other hand, if you become paralyzed with fear, if your palms sweat at just the thought of standing up in the front of the room and singing a song, pushing through that fear is going to be a lot of work. Managing performance anxiety is something that musicians must learn over time.

COMPETITION. Depending on the size of the music program at your college, you might be invited to sing the lead role in the musical, or you might be competing for a minor role with dozens of graduate students. Sometimes competition can be even more intense — and personal — in small programs. Competition is a fact of life, but if you can use it as motivation to work harder rather than as a measure of your value as a person, you'll be happier and more successful in the long run. If you can view competition with your classmates only as an outward expression of the real, inner competition — the one you have with your own potential — then you'll be competing in the right game.

Being a music major is not always fun and hardly ever easy. But wait; there are other reasons NOT to major in music.

Not for the social benefits like in high school

As Frank Battisti has said on many occasions, high school music programs are frequently activity-centered, not music-centered.[7] Trips, festivals, contests, fund-raising events, and sometimes even concerts and rehearsals seem to emphasize the social aspects of music programs. Young people DO need opportunities for social interaction, community-building, and personal growth afforded by school activities; however, when these goals become more import-

7   http://www.youtube.com/watch?v=mzYZb1Z6M74

ant than the teaching and learning of music, the MUSIC program has effectively become a MUSIC ACTIVITIES program. In truth, there's a social aspect to every musical ensemble, from beginners through professionals. The sense of belonging to a community is a basic human need, and high school music programs can fulfill this beautifully.

In college, however, the focus shifts away from peripheral activities to the music itself. Basically, the emphasis changes from learning music in a group to learning music as an individual. You won't have the same kind of "family" as you had in your high school ensemble; or perhaps more accurately, YOUR ROLE in the ensemble changes as you get older, just like it does in your family — from child to adult.

Not because friends and relatives think you're a good singer/instrumentalist

Great musicians get support and encouragement from their family and close friends, but so do average and poor musicians! Assessing musical talent is a fairly objective process (that's what auditions are for), but those closest to you are not objective, nor should they be. Seek out neutral, unbiased expert advice if you're thinking about majoring in music. Your high school music teacher is an excellent source. If you take private lessons (more about this later in Chapter 3), you should pay close attention to what your teacher advises, too.

Not because teaching is a safe fallback career plan

If you think music education is a good major for you because you "can always teach" if your performance/recording career doesn't take off, you're not only shortchanging your performance career, you're probably going to be an unhappy teacher. As challenging as it is to major in music, teaching it in a school is far more demanding. A recent study found that over one-third of entering music teachers have left the profession by their sixth year[8]; other studies put the

---

8   Madsen, Clifford K. and Carl B. Hancock. 2002. Support for music education: A case study of issues concerning teacher retention and attrition. Journal of Research in Music Education 50, no. 1:6-19.

figure above 50%. Reasons for leaving include inadequate budgets, extended working hours, multiple performance expectations, student discipline problems, and lack of administrative support. Don't teach music unless it's your FIRST choice.

Not because you'll make a lot of money

The top earners in any profession make good money, and music is no exception. Members of major symphony orchestras make six figures; recording industry superstars make millions. However, music consistently ranks among the college majors with the lowest-paying average starting salaries. Enough said?

DON'T MAJOR IN MUSIC IF:

YOU CAN'T READ MUSIC. Would you think about majoring in English if you couldn't already read English? Of course not — but every year, students audition for college music programs who can't read music. Since it's quite possible to perform a "successful" audition having learned the music by rote (all too common among singers in particular, but possible on any instrument), too many students begin freshman music theory in the fall who shouldn't. If you can't read music fluently at least at an intermediate level, learn.

YOU CAN'T CARRY A TUNE, EVEN SINGING TO YOURSELF IN THE SHOWER. All musicians sing — the voice is the oldest and most accessible musical instrument. If you think of yourself only as "a [your instrument] player," you won't see the value in learning to sing well. If you begin to see yourself as a musician and artist, however, you will work to develop your voice and ear.

And I don't mean developing operatic vocal technique — a pleasing tone that's not too nasal is enough. The real value lies in developing your ability to sing in tune and with good rhythm, to be expressive, and maybe even to improvise and harmonize a little. If you still can't carry a tune after lots of practice and a bit of help from a music teacher, perhaps you should think about choosing a different major.

YOU'VE NEVER PLAYED THE PIANO OR KEYBOARD (EVEN A LITTLE BIT). There is a piano or electronic keyboard in almost every school in America. Churches, community centers, and many homes have one too. You have the opportunity to become friendly with the keyboard right now, reading both treble and bass clef. Music majors who come to the keyboard for the first time in college have a lot of catching up to do, and it adds to the pressure on them.

YOU STRUGGLE WITH HOMEWORK/READING/WRITING/GRADES IN MOST OF YOUR CLASSES. If getting through high school with decent grades is a challenge, you're going to find the same thing in college, no matter what your major is. If you major in music, you will definitely find the same thing, times two. Classes like music theory and music history require lots of study; courses like ear training, piano, ensembles, and private lessons require lots of practice; and don't forget about those "general education" classes like lab science and Western lit. Music majors have lots of academic pressures, regardless of what some might say.

YOU LISTEN TO ONLY ONE KIND OF MUSIC. Everybody has his or her favorite recording artist or genre, but if your iPod only has one kind of music, you're going to have to expand your tastes; getting a music degree requires learning music that you don't know and maybe won't like. Much of it will grow on you as you become more familiar with it, and you will literally fall in love with some music and have a relationship with it for the rest of your life. Of course, other music you study will never make it to your iPod, and that's OK; your professors don't expect you to like every piece you listen to, study, practice, and perform. What they DO expect is that you recognize and respect its quality.

YOUR HIGH SCHOOL HAS A MUSIC PROGRAM (AND MOST DO), AND YOU'RE NOT INVOLVED IN IT. If you sing or play an instrument, this should be a no-brainer; you ought to be a part of your school chorus, band, or orchestra. If you're a string player and your school does not have an orchestra, you should try to find a community-based youth orchestra in your area. Large ensembles are a mainstay of classical music, and they teach skills you won't learn anywhere else: balance, blend, teamwork, following a conductor, standard repertoire, etc. School music teachers are among the most educated and skilled musicians in the community—learn as much as you can from them by taking every class they teach.

Guitarists and pianists: same advice. Sing in your school chorus or learn an instrument to play in your school band/orchestra, whether you're into classical, rock, pop, or jazz. There's something to learn from every musical experience you have, so give yourself a wide variety of experiences.

YOUR ONLY MUSICAL EXPERIENCES COME FROM YOUR HIGH SCHOOL MUSIC PROGRAM. By the same token, the world is bigger than your high school music program; if you haven't explored it yet, get started now. Perform at your church, in nursing homes, or in a community band/chorus/orchestra or theater. Audition for district and all-state ensembles. Play in a rock band with friends, go to concerts of all kinds, and go to summer music camps. Immerse yourself in as much music as you can find.

YOU WANT TO BE THE NEXT WINNER OF AMERICAN IDOL. If you are seeking fame and fortune through music, America is the land of opportunity—go ahead and seek it! Just don't seek it in a college/university music department. It is abundantly clear which students are there to learn and which are there to impress everyone else (a small percentage, but the most difficult to teach).

ONLY MAJOR IN MUSIC IF:

- ☑ You have musical aptitude/ability/talent.
- ☑ You can't see yourself possibly doing anything else.
- ☑ You have determination, a "fire in the belly."
- ☑ You enjoy spending a lot of time alone.
- ☑ You're able to accomplish things when you're alone.
- ☑ You also enjoy working with people.

☑ You're able to get along with people who are very different from you.

☑ You're able to delay gratification.

☑ You don't need material possessions or lots of money to be happy.

☑ You're able to admit your mistakes and learn from them.

So, if you still want to major in music, let's get to the details. But first, a few words for the adults in your life.

CHAPTER **2** | For Parents,
Guidance Counselors,
and Teachers

Raising children is an uncertain thing;
success is reached only after a life of battle
and worry.

— DEMOCRITUS

If you're reading this chapter (and maybe the rest of this book) because you're an adult with a son/daughter/student who's told you they want to major in music, and you're not sure how to process that bombshell, take a deep breath. It's going to be OK.

AS A PARENT, WHAT CAN I DO TO HELP MY SON/DAUGHTER PREPARE FOR A COLLEGE MUSIC MAJOR?

Provide support for private lessons.

Private lessons — ideally, three or four years in high school — are an essential part of preparing to major in music (please read Chapter 3), and each family manages the expense according to its own resources. Often lessons are directly paid for by the parents, but in many families the cost is shared between parents, relatives, and the student him/herself. Some school music booster organizations offer partial scholarships for private study to students who are members of the school band, orchestra, or choir; ask your child's teacher if this is the case at your school. Some private teachers, especially those connected with a non-profit community music school, may offer to charge on a sliding scale, based on the family's ability to pay. Remember, though, that in many cases the private teacher makes a living as a musician through lots of different (and unpredictable) sources, and teaching private lessons is an important and relatively stable source of income. If you and your son/daughter commit to taking private lessons with someone, make sure to attend every lesson.

How do you find a good private teacher? Start by asking your child's school music teacher for his or her recommendation. If you live close enough to a college or university, find out if their faculty teach high school students privately; many do, or can recommend a colleague or former student who does. Many cities and towns have a community music center. Local music stores often hire private teachers to give lessons in their store, and some school music teachers also teach private lessons in their "spare" time. There are even online private teacher locators, though they tend to be incomplete. Those living in rural areas will likely have to travel farther, but teachers ARE out there.

Provide a quality instrument.

The woodwind, brass, string, or percussion instrument your son or daughter probably played as a beginner was designed and manufactured to provide a good start to their music education. It makes sense to begin with an affordable and durable instrument, but students often outgrow the limitations of a "beginner model" within a few years. Many manufacturers have even created a "step-up" line of instruments to fill this intermediate need. As their physical and musical skills grow, however, serious high school musicians will discover the difference a professional instrument makes. The craftsmanship and materials in a quality instrument allow for a richer, more flexible tone quality, smoother technique, wider range from soft to loud, and greater ability to play in tune.

Professional models vary widely in price, based on the type of instrument, manufacturer, and age; sometimes an excellent used instrument is a better choice than a new one. Your child's private teacher is the best resource for help in choosing an instrument, so take your time, do the research, have your child's teacher play the instrument, and choose wisely according to your family's budget.

Take an active role in your child's school music activities.

Because of the public nature of musical performances and the many activities surrounding school music programs, it's a lot easier to learn about your child's passion for music than it would be in most other academic areas (since there were no math concerts, I never did understand what my oldest son found so fascinating about calculus). Most high school music programs have a "music booster" organization that helps with fund-raising, chaperoning on trips, serving as ushers at concerts, and dozens of other tasks. If you're not already actively involved, volunteer as much time as you can, go to meetings, and ask your child's school music teacher how you can help. Seeing the "behind-the-scenes" workings of a school music program can help you understand why your child loves this so much; you'll also get to know some of the greatest people in the school in music teachers, students, and other parents. Of course, also attend as many of your child's concerts and performances as you can. They may not always tell you, but it means a lot to them.

Encourage solo and ensemble performances.

Another facet of school music that holds great value for aspiring musicians is the solo and ensemble festival. These are usually organized by state and local music educators' organizations, college music departments, or other educational groups. In contrast to being in a large band/orchestra/choir, rehearsing and performing a solo or a small chamber piece places much more responsibility on the individual, and it is a powerful method for advancing musical independence, as well as learning how to collaborate with other musicians. Solo and ensemble performances are a staple of college music study. They're also a lot of fun.

Provide support for music activities outside of school.

It's extremely important for prospective music majors to participate in music activities outside of school, including district and all-state festivals, community music school ensembles, and summer music camps. These are the first places where they can "test" themselves against other high-achieving student musicians in the larger world to see how they measure up, and if they enjoy the faster pace and higher expectations of serious music-making.

Encourage them to do well in all their high school classes.

Unfortunately, some students who audition successfully for potential acceptance into a college music program are not admitted because they don't meet the college's minimum academic requirements for high school grades, SAT scores, or required college-prep classes. I see this happen each year, and it's a painful experience for everyone. College music programs do not have the "pull" with their school's admissions office that big-time athletic programs sometimes do, nor should they; majoring in music is academically challenging (please read Chapter One).

When necessary, advocate for your child's right to enroll in the music classes he or she wants and needs.

If your son or daughter is contemplating studying music in college, the benefit of continuous music enrollment throughout high school can't be overstated. It's actually good for ANY student in the high school program, but doubly so for prospective music majors.

Administrators and guidance counselors spend weeks each summer constructing a school-wide schedule that allows students to take the courses they need and want — it's an unbelievably complicated process. Despite their best efforts, however, sometimes students get hit with a conflict between music and some other course, and they're told they can't take music. Often the other course is an honors/AP section that is only offered once in the schedule (known as a "singleton" class), and students are told they need it for college. If this happens, talk with your child's guidance counselor to see what can be worked out. Maybe the other class can be taken another semester (or year) when it won't conflict, or maybe — and I say this very carefully — it's not "required."

Every high school has its minimum course requirements for graduation, and of course taking these is not open to discussion (although WHEN they are taken might be). All high schools also identify the courses that college-bound students SHOULD take, but these are recommendations — based on what "most" colleges require for entrance. Do ALL colleges require four years of English? Pretty much. Three years of the same foreign language? Not all. Four years of math? It depends. And so on. I AM NOT advocating a light academic load for anyone — but before your son or daughter enrolls in a recommended course which conflicts with music, I do suggest that you perform some research on your own on college admissions websites where your son/daughter might apply. There may be some room between what the colleges actually require and what your high school recommends, and this may be where that music course can fit.

Let them succeed (or not) on their own.

Supporting your child in a musical career isn't the same as being their producer or agent. Encourage them to practice, but don't nag. Talk about their performances with them, but don't be critical. Have serious discussions with them about their college options, but let THEM ask most of the questions on campus visits. They will love you for it.

As a music teacher, I sometimes had a hard time taking this approach with my own sons when they were growing up, and in hindsight, I can see where I pushed too hard. Teaching music at the college where one of them is a music major has added to the challenge, since evaluating his musical and scholastic performance on a regular basis is part of my job. I am also quite aware of his potential, but I knew I had to tread carefully. I even made sure one of my colleagues was his academic advisor rather than myself, just to give us more space to work out our changing roles. Happily, my son asked me to be his advisor after a couple years, and we eventually figured out how to talk both as father/son and as professor/student.

If you're ambivalent about their decision to major in music, make your point, but try to go with the flow.

My high school grades were good — AP classes, National Honor Society, and so on — and for most of my childhood I wanted to be a physician like my father. Although I definitely had some friends who thought my eventual choice of a music career was cool, there were some (I found out 30 years later at my reunion) who couldn't believe I became a musician instead of a doctor. They thought it was a "waste."

On the other hand, when I told my parents (around my junior year in high school) that I was more interested in majoring in music than in pre-med, my dad's only negative comment was, "You know, a lot of doctors at the hospital play music on the weekends. . . ." That was a pretty mild suggestion that I should keep pre-med as an option (which I did only until I was a month into my freshman year as a music major), and I'm forever grateful that they supported my choice.

Most parents want to support their children's academic choices, but they're concerned how their adult children will earn a living. Many times what appears to be ambivalence about majoring in music is really concern about the future. We just want our children to be independent, happy, and fabulously wealthy. I understand: my oldest son is a mechanical engineer, and my youngest is a music major.

Get informed and "network."

Websites such as College Confidential[9], GreatSchools[10], and College Blog[11] provide lots of information about various college majors, including music. Parent forums on these sites are great places to hear first-hand about auditions, application procedures, and the general concerns of college parents.

---

9 http://www.collegeconfidential.com/
10 http://www.greatschools.org/
11 http://collegeblog.positionu4college.com/

Understand the real benefits of studying music.

Most people have heard of "the Mozart effect," but there's a lot of hyperbole surrounding this topic.[12] In the original research, college students who listened to ten minutes of a Mozart piano concerto scored higher on a test of spatial reasoning, taken immediately after, than those who didn't. This rather narrow outcome took on a life of its own, however, as popular media began touting this as a way to make children "smarter." Books and recordings were marketed to anxious parents, the news media had a new headline-grabbing story, and the governor of Georgia even gave free a Mozart CD to every expectant mother in his state. Although lots of subsequent studies sought to replicate effects found in the original study, results were very inconsistent. It is now generally accepted that the "Mozart effect" does not exist. Passively listening to classical music won't raise your SAT's.

The study of music can, however, make you a more interesting person. Our society places inordinate value on good looks and physical attractiveness, but most of our success in life — from business to personal relationships — is the result of our ability to interact with others. Ultimately, it is our personality that determines whether people are attracted to us or shy away from us. And an education in the arts is one of humanity's oldest and most esteemed forms of personal development.

Ancient Greek and Roman civilizations put great emphasis on the study of music. Philosophers such as Aristotle believed that music, as an expression of the mathematical laws that govern the universe, was a force that also affected the universe — specifically, human moral and ethical behavior — therefore, its place in the curriculum was taken very seriously. In Medieval times, educated people (i.e., men who studied to become priests) were instructed in the basics of composition and harmony, as well as singing and the playing of instruments.

Many of history's most influential people — Goethe, Martin Luther, Thomas Jefferson, Abraham Lincoln, Gandhi — had a deep and

12 http://en.wikipedia.org/wiki/Mozart_effect

abiding love of the arts, though it was not what the world knew them for. John Adams, our nation's second president and one of the Founding Fathers, is famously quoted as writing to his wife: "I must study politics and war, that our sons may have liberty to study mathematics and philosophy, in order to give their children a right to study painting, poetry, and music."

What these great minds realized was that study and practice of the fine arts elevate the human spirit and nourish the soul. Although the performance of music requires great physical coordination, and its study demands cognitive reasoning at a high level, music's greatest value is its ability to embody and express that which is BEYOND actions and words. All great art transcends time, place, and the movement of thought to connect with the stillness of the present moment that exists in each of us. Bennett Reimer referred to this as "affect" or "feelingfulness." Abraham Maslow called these "peak experiences." Great music is transparent to transcendence — it allows one to see through it to something beyond this world. As Douglas Adams, author of "A Hitchhiker's Guide to the Galaxy" writes, "Beethoven tells you what it's like to be Beethoven and Mozart tells you what it's like to be human. Bach tells you what it's like to be the universe." In a sense, though, all great music "tells you what it's like to be the universe," and the deeper one's experience is with great music, through determined study and practice, the deeper his or her experience is with life itself.

AS A HIGH SCHOOL GUIDANCE COUNSELOR, WHAT CAN I DO TO HELP PROSPECTIVE MUSIC MAJORS?

Communicate with middle school music students who are coming to your school next year.

Make sure incoming freshmen are aware of the choices they have for high school electives, including music classes. To do this, of course, you need to be very familiar with the music offerings at your high school, as well as the musical skills and experience that your music teachers will expect from incoming freshmen. High school music programs don't succeed in isolation; they are part of a comprehensive

K-12 music program, and they depend on students making a smooth transition from middle to high school. Many times the high school music teachers will also work to ensure this happens by visiting the middle school music classes, talking about the high school music ensembles, and encouraging students to enroll in them.

Get to know the music teachers in your school, and be familiar with the various components of their program.

Meet with your music teachers once a year and find out more about their program. Ask them how you can be of assistance in identifying potential music students and in helping maintain the music program's health. The most recognizable activities (e.g., marching band, Broadway musicals) often overshadow the core elements of the program (e.g., concert band, choir); but these core classes require most of the music teacher's time and attention. Other elements such as solo/ensemble festivals and private lessons get almost no attention from people outside the music department, but they are vital components to a comprehensive program.

Help maintain continuous enrollment in the proper music classes for students in grades 9 through 12.

For students who are a part of the sequential, skill-based curricula of band, orchestra, and choir, continuous enrollment in the appropriate classes in grades 9-12 is a very important factor. Problems can occur when students are kept out because of a class conflict, or when students are enrolled in a music class without possessing the requisite skills. Music is unlike most other high school subjects, where students enroll in different classes through the years (e.g., Algebra I, Algebra II, Trigonometry, Calculus). The student enrolling in the same "Band" class for four years DOES NOT have the same experience every year; as their skills grow, they learn more about music and are held to higher standards. (Though they may not advertise it, music teachers are masters of "individualized instruction.") In addition, the core musical repertoire that's rehearsed, studied, and performed in each ensemble is often planned on a four-year rotation, so that new learning takes place every year in the same ensemble.

Furthermore, music ensembles require specialized skills from students on various instruments, much like a football team requires some defensive backs, some offensive linemen, a quarterback, and so on. A music ensemble with balanced instrumentation is vital—it enhances the educational experience for ALL students. If the oboe player can't enroll in band because it conflicts with AP Chemistry, the entire band suffers, not just that one student.

If at all possible, schedule students into music classes first, then other singleton classes.
Conflicts between advanced/AP courses and music courses are quite likely, because many students are in both, and I have never seen a successful high school music program that did not have this vital support from the school administration and guidance department.

Understand the necessity, and the procedures, for college auditions.
Auditions are required for entrance into all good college programs because they care about your students' success. College music programs are demanding, and it would be wrong to accept students into a program for which they do not show potential for musical success. An audition clearly reveals this.

Usually, the audition process is handled (by the music department) independently of the admissions process. If a student winds up denied admission to the college, the audition becomes irrelevant, of course—but being admitted to XYZ College does not mean the student can simply declare music as their major. Information on scheduling an audition is usually easily available on the college music department website.

Make sure prospective music majors contact the music department at schools they're applying to, not just the admissions office. Communication between the admissions office and the music department, regarding perhaps hundreds of prospective majors, is not always seamless. Despite my best efforts, every fall a few freshmen who have not auditioned show up on our rosters as "music majors." Most often, these students have had no counseling and very little musical guidance, they do not pass the audition that is set up at the last minute (if one even is), and the whole college entrance process becomes a disaster.

Learn where the good college music programs are in your area and provide guidance in the selection of schools to which students should apply.

Talk to your music teachers; they're probably well acquainted with good college music programs. Don't just go by online search engines, or even college websites; simply offering a major in music is entirely different than having a quality program.

Be prepared for that student who is a "diamond in the rough."

Some students, particularly those from lower-income families, may not have had the same opportunities to flourish academically and musically as others — but they possess the potential to succeed in a structured college musical environment. By all means, talk with your school music teachers to get their assessment if you think you have such an individual. Help him or her look for the right college music program — the prestigious (and expensive) college music programs may not necessarily be the best choice. Smaller programs, where the student won't get lost in the crowd, may be a better choice. Learn what music education resources exist outside of your school for low-income families in your community, too. Students and parents may be unaware of a community music school whose tuition is based on the family's ability to pay, for example.

Notify students of music scholarship opportunities.

In addition to general academic scholarships awarded through the admissions office, nearly all college music programs offer music scholarships to the most talented students, based on their audition performance. These can range from one-shot awards of a few hundred dollars, up to full tuition renewable for four years. Information on music scholarships is usually easy to find on music department websites, as it's a major component of their recruiting efforts. In addition, inform students about any local scholarships in your community for which they might be eligible, including those specifically in music.

Provide brochures and university publications to various music schools.

Even in the digital age, students (and parents) respond to print media. Make sure it's displayed where students can see it and take it home. If you run out of space to display every poster you get from college music departments, ask your music teachers if they would like to post some in the music room.

Ensure students meet all application and audition deadlines.

It's frustrating for students when they miss important deadlines, like the final audition day at their top- choice college.

AS A HIGH SCHOOL MUSIC TEACHER, WHAT CAN I DO TO HELP PREPARE FUTURE MUSIC MAJORS?

Build the most balanced, comprehensive, and rigorous music program possible for ALL students.

It's not easy; it takes musical talent, people skills, sustained effort, and perpetual willingness to learn. But when the realization comes that you actually make a difference in the lives of your students, what other options do you really have?

None of us has the "perfect" job, but a wise person said, "You may think the grass is greener on the other side, but if you take the time to water your own grass, it would be just as green." Water your grass by showing your students the way to develop good musical fundamentals of pitch, rhythm, tone, and technique. Play great music that nourishes the soul; music that enlightens, not just entertains. Find that sweet spot in each rehearsal that balances being demanding with being satisfied. Do your best to provide leadership in all facets of your music program: large ensembles, jazz, solo and chamber music opportunities, individual instruction, music theory and literature, composition, and service to the community that supports your program.

Build the quality of your program before trying to build its size; otherwise, quality will never happen. Unfortunately, programs can also experience growth by SACRIFICING quality, appealing only to students' desire for "fun." Emphasis on size at the expense of quality deprives ALL students, not just prospective music majors, of deep and meaningful music learning in high school. A high-quality program will attract students in time.

That said, the size of your program matters a great deal to administrators and guidance personnel when scheduling classes. It's no secret why larger singleton classes tend to get scheduled first; if AP English has 25 students and only one of them is in band, the entire school schedule won't be re-worked if these courses conflict. Over time, aim to build a program that is big enough to warrant the scheduling priority that will benefit your students.

Go for intrinsic.

Students learn more than music from you; they learn values. It's a sad fact that the overwhelming majority of students who are active in high school music programs don't continue to play or sing once they graduate. Of course, life is full of choices — but students who continue their relationship with music after high school have learned that it's something they don't want to be without. To them, the sacrifices of time, effort, and money are worth the rewards they get from making music. What kinds of rewards are your students learning? For example, does the value of marching band lie in winning competitions, or in longer-lasting rewards, such as your students knowing they have given something unique back to their community?

As you may remember from Educational Psychology 101, when external rewards stop, the behaviors that were being rewarded also cease. In his 2011 best seller *Drive*[13], Daniel Pink goes so far as to

13 http://www.youtube.com/watch?feature=player_embedded&v=u6XAPnuFjJc

show that external rewards even DIMINISH performance in complex cognitive skills. It's difficult for high school students to learn to love music for its own sake, and to carry that love throughout their lives, when music programs over-emphasize the external rewards of trophies, competition, and trips to theme parks. When these activities are over after high school, it's the intrinsic rewards that keep people active as amateur (or professional) musicians. Teach students to love music, not just the activity of band, orchestra, or chorus.

Encourage and monitor academic excellence in your students.
Do your band/orchestra/chorus students receive recognition for their scholastic achievements in music classes, as well as in their other classes? Many high schools have a Tri-M chapter or some other club whose purposes are to acknowledge high-achieving music students and to provide opportunities for service and leadership in their school music program. Eligibility could be based on a combination of musicianship, contribution to the music program, and grades in all classes. Equating students' musical achievement with academic recognition reinforces the concept that dedicated music study is an academic, as well as an artistic, undertaking.

Work to earn the trust and good will of your school guidance department.
Administrative support for your program begins with the guidance department. Guidance counselors are on the front line when it comes to administrators who can help your program reach its goals.

Hold a yearly information night early in the fall for prospective music majors and their parents.
You're the expert—you succeeded as a music major! Share your knowledge and experience with prospective music majors and their parents at a presentation each fall. Invite all juniors and seniors in your school who are contemplating majoring in music, and don't forget to reach out to students who may not be in your program. Help students and parents understand application and audition procedures, speak about the demands of being a college music major,

inform them of scholarship opportunities at colleges and in your community, and answer questions.

Help students apply to colleges and prepare for auditions.
High school seniors who intend to major in music should have repertoire of two or three major solos/etudes prepared for college auditions. Listen to their audition pieces, offer constructive feedback, talk about what kind of college music programs would be a good match for them, talk with them about what they want to do AFTER college, and write those letters of recommendation.

CHAPTER **3** | Your Instrument/Voice

Spock: The needs of the many outweigh
the needs of the few.
Kirk: Or the one.

Private Lessons

In most school music programs, the focus is naturally on the large ensembles that form the core of the curriculum; Spock and Kirk would probably feel right at home (at least philosophically) in band, orchestra, or chorus. In fact, the development of class methods of instrument instruction, allowing one teacher to instruct many students at once, has brought band and orchestra music into the lives of more young people than at any other time in history, and the story of American music education in the twentieth century is in large part the story of these ensembles.[14]

Most vocal music in schools is also learned in a large ensemble setting, and these roots go back much further. Guitar classes are becoming increasingly popular, and even group piano classes are making inroads in many schools, using technology that allows one teacher to manage over a dozen piano students at once.

---

14 Humphreys, Jere. (1989). An Overview of American Public School Bands and Orchestras before World War II. Bulletin of the Council for Research in Music Education, 101, pp. 50-60.

While group methods of music instruction may have broadened music education's coverage across American culture, nothing can ever replace the depth of musical discovery available in private, one-on-one lessons. There is simply no substitute for the individualized listening, analysis, and feedback by a competent private teacher. This form of mentoring/apprenticeship has been the model for music teaching and learning since the dawn of music, and all college music programs require it, with good reason. It is the crucible in the laboratory of music where the apprentice, teacher, instrument, and literature are combined under heat and pressure for a period of time each week to produce permanent change in the student.[15]

This is the first and by far the most important step in preparing to major in music: study with the best private teacher available, begin as early as possible, and follow their advice and instruction with as much dedication as you can.

What can a private teacher do for you that can't be learned in band, orchestra, or chorus? For starters, you will be exposed to a whole new repertoire of music. If you only go to Italian restaurants, you'll never discover sushi; if you only read American novels, you'll never enjoy Shakespeare. There is a wealth of fantastic music written for solo voice and every instrument that you'll never be exposed to in large ensembles, and this music forms the core of private lessons. A good private teacher knows this repertoire inside and out, and will select the most appropriate music for you, based on your current ability and areas needing improvement.

What happens in private lessons? Like a baseball pitching coach, a good private teacher will assess your skills accurately, diagnose problems that may be interfering with your performance, and hold you accountable for correcting these problems through practice. There will be a balance of critical listening to your performance, discussion, and occasional singing/playing by the teacher. A variety of technical exercises, etudes, and solos will be assigned to you, and

15 Kennell, Richard. (2002). New Handbook of Research in Music Teaching and Learning [Richard Colwell, ed.]. MENC. p.252.

your progress over the weeks, months, and years will be carefully assessed. It is simply impossible for your band, orchestra, or chorus director to do this for everyone in his or her large ensemble at the level of detail needed by those who aspire to major in music.

In addition to developing musical knowledge and skills, most students develop strong personal connections with their private teacher. A great teacher serves not just as a model for what to sound like, but also as a source of inspiration in difficult times, a friend who does not sugar-coat the truth, and a supportive mentor.

How do you find a good private teacher? Start by asking your school music teacher. If you like the way someone plays or sings, ask them who their private teacher is. No matter how you find private teachers, make sure you try them on for size — go to one lesson just to see how the "chemistry" is between you and the teacher. If you're not entirely satisfied after a period of time, try another teacher; but also give the relationship a fair chance. The best teachers have high standards, and sometimes this might feel like they don't "like you." Don't worry about that, just do what your teacher says and come to your lessons prepared — practice!

Practice Habits

Despite their value outlined above, taking private lessons won't "teach" you how to play music. In a very practical sense, YOU are your only teacher. Day after day, you are the only person who will decide to actually get started with practice time, to keep practicing as much as you should, to work on what you know you should, to listen to yourself and evaluate how you sound, and to set clear and detailed goals for what you want to accomplish. These are the gifts you bring to your private teacher at each lesson, and he/she will hear it — and love it!

As much as possible, set aside a regular time each day for practice; if that time is busy on a given day, practice when you can. Practice somewhere that's free of distractions like other people, the TV, and the computer, and leave your cell phone in another room. Keep your instrument, music, and accessories together in one place at the end of each session so they're ready for the next time. For heaven's sake, don't keep your instrument on the shelf at school.

How much should you practice? Answering this simple question is not so simple — your teacher will have a better idea of what you need. Twenty minutes a day was good when you were a beginner, but college music majors typically practice two or more hours a day. Two or three half-hour sessions spread throughout the day are much more effective than one marathon session. (Helpful Tip: If your parents often have to remind you to practice, maybe you're not serious enough about music to major in it.)

Have a plan each time you practice. The worst thing you can do (besides not practicing at all) is to sit down, take out your instrument, and begin playing whatever comes to your mind until you're tired, repeating the same thing at the same tempo — and likely making the same mistakes. Here are some tips for effective practice:

- ☑ Each day should include a balance of maintenance, technique, etudes, ensemble and solo repertoire, sight-reading, improvisation, and fun.

- ☑ Don't practice what you already are good at, practice what you're not; be willing to sound pretty awful for at least thirty minutes a day.

- ☑ Keep a journal with your music to jot down observations and questions for your teacher at your next lesson.

- ☑ Use a metronome each day and write tempos on the music (http://www.metronomeonline.com/).

- ☑ Play EVERYTHING with rock-solid rhythm; especially don't cheat the long notes.

- ☑ Play or sing with a drone to improve your intonation (http://www.idrs.org/multimedia/midi/PUB/Drones.htm).

- ☑ If a passage is technically difficult, slow it down — way down. Go slow enough to play it perfectly many times.

- ☑ Don't practice something until you can do it right — practice it until you can't do it wrong.

- ☑ Never sacrifice tone for technique or speed — play or sing everything with your best possible sound.

- ☑ Playing and singing softly is much harder than doing it loudly; practice your soft dynamics a lot.

- ☑ Play or sing everything with musical expression, even the most mundane technical drills. Don't just go for the notes, go for the musical meaning BEHIND the notes. Give every phrase a beginning, middle, and end.

The ability to perform music accurately and expressively as a soloist is the touchstone that demonstrates your musical potential; it is no coincidence that all good college music programs require a performance audition for entrance. In college, private lessons are called "applied music" because solo performance is where you apply all the knowledge gained in theory, ear training, history, and analysis. At its core, music is a PERFORMING art — this is true whether you want to teach it, perform it, compose it, study it, or write about it. Hours and hours in the practice room will make you a better musician, and there is no shortcut. Begin now.

> "At the age of 30 I decided to get my Water Safety Instructor rating. After one of the tests, the teacher pulled me aside and asked, 'I need to know something. I watch you in the pool practicing and you look like one of the weakest swimmers in the class, but when I take out the clipboard and rate you, you're one of the best. What is going on?' I explained that I was a music major, and when I'm practicing I'm going over what I'm weakest at, and when you are rating me I'm applying the practice."
>
> — Glenn E. Giles, Castleton State College, VT

CHAPTER 4 | Music Theory

Curiosity begins as an act of tearing to pieces or analysis.

— SAMUEL ALEXANDER

Music isn't just something to perform. It's not a random arrangement of pitches and rhythms; it has organization, internal logic, and form. In many ways, music is the way math would sound if you could hear it. When we engage our intellect with music (using the left brain), its architecture becomes apparent and more of its beauty is revealed. These insights not only deepen our appreciation when we listen to music; they also shape our performances and allow us to be more musically expressive. Studying music at the college level involves a great deal of musical analysis, but most incoming music majors lack experience and fundamental skills in this area.

After private lessons, the next most important step in preparing to major in music is to learn the fundamentals of music theory. Most college music programs require at least two years of theory, and most students find them to be fast-paced, difficult, and at times extremely frustrating. Starting with the basics well in hand is like being in good physical shape when running a marathon — it won't make it easy, but it WILL make it a lot easier. The reason has to do with the concept of *automaticity*.

Automaticity

The term "automaticity" refers to the ability to perform a complex task so expertly that the conscious mind no longer is involved in its details and can attend to other, more abstract issues. On a purely physical level, walking is an excellent example of this state of mind. Intellectual tasks can also reach the state of automaticity: right now you're reading this sentence without sounding out each individual word like you did when you were learning to read, and you can attend more closely to its meaning. In music theory, the skills that need this level of automaticity are identification of notes in the treble and bass clefs, ability to spell all major scales and identify their key signatures, and identification and spelling of intervals and triads.

Clefs

Most high school musicians are familiar with either treble or bass clef. If you read music in only one of these, you are in the majority, so don't be discouraged. However, you'll soon be expected to read and write in both on a daily basis, so learn the names of the lines and spaces now. There is an excellent lesson at http://www.musictheory.net/lessons/10. Then, practice reading music in the clef where you're least comfortable. There's plenty of free sheet music in all clefs on the Web (http://www.8notes.com/, for instance). Pick an easy tune written in an unfamiliar clef, and play it on your instrument, in whatever octave is appropriate.

When a treble clef and a bass clef staff are joined on the left by a bracket and line like this,

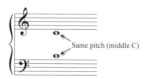

Same pitch (middle C)

it's called the grand staff, and it covers about three octaves. Middle C sits between the two staves as either the first ledger line below the treble clef or the first ledger line above the bass clef. The grand staff is what pianists use most often, and you'll be using it for almost all of your music theory assignments.

Major Scales

Nowhere is music's internal logic more obvious than in the construction and spelling of major scales and their associated key signatures. "Know all your major scales" is excellent advice you've probably heard before, but there are different levels of "knowing." You should be able to play all major scales from memory on your instrument in one or two octaves (vocalists, you should be able to play them at the piano), AND you should be able to spell them out loud. For example, if I asked you to spell the D-flat major scale, you should be able to say fairly rapidly (without thinking before each note) "five flats: D-flat, E-flat, F, G-flat, A-flat, B-flat, C, D-flat."

So how should you learn them? A lot depends on your own learning style. Some people prefer a straight-ahead, grind-it-out memorization by reading, spelling, and playing each scale (http://www.teoria.com/tutorials/scales/sc-tool.php). Others find the pattern of whole-steps and half steps shared by all major scales an easy way to begin (http://www.musictheorysite.com/major-scales/). Some people prefer thinking in terms of key signatures; for instance, naming the scales in order of increasing number of flats or sharps in their key signature (http://www.musictheory.net/lessons/25). For lessons on building the major scales, go to http://www.musictheory.net/lessons/21, http://www.neiu.edu/~jalucas/muscon/lectures/scale/index.htm, or http://www.teoria.com/tutorials/scales/index.php.

Regardless of the methods you choose, the ultimate goals are the same: instantaneous recognition of key signatures, and the ability to spell and play all major scales quickly. This takes LOTS of sustained and patient effort (i.e., practice), and there is no shortcut. Sorry. But on the other hand, it's not really hard. You WILL improve rather quickly once you begin daily practice. For exercises, go to http://www.teoria.com/exercises/sc.php, http://www.musictheory.net/exercises, or http://www.emusictheory.com/practice/scales.html.

Scale Degrees

Since all major scales have the same pattern of half steps and whole steps (and thus have the same "shape"), it's often helpful to refer to their steps, or degrees, with generic names. The first note of a scale is often called the tonic note, or just "tonic." Leonard Bernstein referred to it as the "home plate" of music — you start out there, you run to the other bases (notes of the scale), but the whole point is to get back to home.

The following illustration uses the C major scale, but the names of the scale degrees apply to ALL major scales. The different systems for naming scale degrees can be used interchangeably.

| $\hat{1}$ | $\hat{2}$ | $\hat{3}$ | $\hat{4}$ | $\hat{5}$ | $\hat{6}$ | $\hat{7}$ | $\hat{1}$ |
| Tonic | Supertonic | Mediant | Subdominant | Dominant | Submediant | Leading Tone | Tonic |

When given a scale degree and a major key (e.g., "dominant in F Major"), you should be able to name the note quickly (the answer is "C"). More useful, however, is the ability to identify the scale degree when given the major key signature and the pitch. For example, consider the note C-sharp, with four sharps in the key signature. Four sharps in a major key means E major, and C-sharp is $\hat{6}$ (or submediant) in that key. Here's another: three flats in the major key, and the note is F. The answer is at the bottom of the page[16]. You can learn more about scale degrees at http://www.musictheory.net/lessons/23. A great place to practice identification of scale degrees is http://pedaplus.com/games/degrees/.

Major and Minor Scales

Once major scales are well in hand (but don't wait too long), it's an easy step to learn minor scales. Each major scale has a minor scale (called its relative minor) with the exact same key signature — but the tonic note is different. Returning to Bernstein's baseball analogy,

---

16 F is $\hat{2}$, or supertonic in E flat major.

it's like you're playing in the same ballpark, running the same bases, but hitting from (and trying to get back to) third base instead of home plate.

The submediant (6̂) in each major scale is tonic of that key's relative minor. For example, B-flat major's relative minor key is G minor, because G is the submediant (6̂) in B-flat major. As you can see, every key signature designates both a major key and its relative minor; for example, a key signature with three flats indicates either E-flat major OR C minor. Learning how to tell the difference when looking at a piece of music is part of college music theory; but for now you should know key signatures in both major and minor.

You should also learn to spell all minor scales (in natural, harmonic, and melodic forms). Learn more about minor scales at http://www.musictheory.net/lessons/22 and http://www.teoria.com/tutorials/scales/index.php, and practice them at http://www.emusictheory.com/practice/scales.html or http://www.teoria.com/exercises/sc.php.

Intervals

The distance in pitch between two notes is called the "interval," and it's the next theory fundamental to master after your scales. Most freshman music majors are at least familiar with major and minor scales, and many know them quite well; however, those who are already adept at intervals quickly work their way to the top of the music theory grading curve, and they tend to stay there.

After years of teaching freshman theory, the reason is clear to me: the identification and spelling of intervals pervades EVERY SINGLE corner of music theory. If your intervals are at the level of automaticity (see above), your mind can concentrate on more complex issues. If it takes too much time to identify and spell intervals however, tasks like harmonic analysis become overwhelming. Flash cards — or the online equivalent — are a great learning tool. Accuracy counts, of course — but speed counts too. So test yourself and push yourself, just like an athlete would do.

You must be able to identify intervals (name the interval between two given pitches) and spell intervals (name the note that's a given interval either above or below a given starting note). For example, a major third above C is E, and a major third below it is A-flat.

Confused? That's OK. Discouraged? Don't be. Like everything else, it takes time, lots of practice, and attention to details. There are plenty of places on the web to learn and practice intervals: http://www.musictheory.net/exercises, http://www.teoria.com/exercises/index.php, and http://www.emusictheory.com/practice.html are good places to begin. Give yourself timed tests twice a week, increasing the difficulty level until you're identifying and spelling all major, minor, perfect, diminished, and augmented intervals up to one octave. Your goal should be twenty questions in one minute, with an accuracy of 90% or better.

Triads

The triad forms the building block of traditional harmony; it is a set of three pitches stacked in major or minor thirds. The most important member of the triad, and the one whose pitch is used in naming the triad, is called the root (e.g., the root of the G major triad is the note G). The next member is a major or minor third above the root, and it's called (surprisingly enough) the third of the triad. The fifth of the triad is a perfect, diminished, or augmented fifth above the root. And that's it—but depending on the particular combination of major/minor third and perfect/diminished/augmented fifth, the quality (or "flavor") of the triad varies dramatically. The four most common qualities are listed as follows, with examples using C as the root.

Major	Root — C
	Third — Major third above root (E)
	Fifth — Perfect fifth above root (G)
Minor	Root — C
	Third — Minor third above root (E flat)
	Fifth — Perfect fifth above root (G)

Diminished	Root — C
	Third — Minor third above root (E flat)
	Fifth — Diminished fifth above root (G flat)
Augmented	Root — C
	Third — Major third above root (E)
	Fifth — Augmented fifth above root (G sharp)

As you can begin to see, becoming fluent in spelling and identifying triads depends entirely on being fluent in spelling and identifying intervals (which, in turn, depends on your fluency with scales and key signatures). So what are you waiting for? Go to http://www.musictheory.net/exercises, http://www.teoria.com/exercises/index.php, and http://www.emusictheory.com/practice.html, and start practicing! As with intervals, your goal should be twenty questions in one minute, with an accuracy of 90% or better.

Where's the Root?

Here's a question that may seem impossible to answer, but it's not. What's the root of the following triad: note X, note Y, or note Z?

Even with no clef sign, and thus no pitch names, it's possible to solve this riddle. Big Hint: don't assume it's the one on the bottom. Remember, a triad is a set of three pitches stacked in thirds; or in other words, there must be the root, a third above the root, and a fifth above the root. The example above has a fourth and a sixth above note X, so that one, by definition, can't be the root. However, can you rearrange the triad by moving one note an octave up or down to form a stack of thirds?

If note X is shifted up one octave to this,

it's clear that note Y sits at the bottom of a stack of thirds (it has a third above and a fifth above), and it is the root of this generic mystery triad. Cheating? Not at all. **The lowest note of a triad is not always the root.**

Inversions of Triads

A father, mother, and baby are traveling down the highway, and as you pass their car you glance over and look in their car. No matter who's driving, you'd be able to identity the three pretty easily, right? (In our little story, let's say even the baby could be behind the wheel!) Regardless of who's sitting where, their identities and their roles in the family don't change. In a very similar way, the identity and function of members of a triad don't change, regardless of their arrangement on the staff. But, like the driver's seat in a car, the lowest note in a triad has special significance.

A triad whose lowest note isn't the root (i.e., the third or the fifth of the triad is the lowest note) is said to be "inverted." Rearranging the notes in a triad like this doesn't change its root or its quality (major, minor, diminished, augmented), but it does alter the "shading" and stability of the triad in subtle ways. You'll learn how to use inversions in college music theory, but the fundamental skill to develop now is the recognition and spelling of triads in root position and in inversions.

When the root of the triad (e.g., the pitch C in a C major triad) is the lowest note, the triad is said to be in "root position." It's the most common, and the most stable, position. It doesn't matter how the third and the fifth are distributed above, as long as the root is at the bottom. Here are several examples of a C major triad in root position:

When the third of a triad (e.g., the pitch E in a C major triad) is the lowest note, the triad is said to be in "first inversion." It's fairly common in classical harmony (much less so in jazz and rock), and it is less stable than root position. It's never found at the end of a piece for instance — but it has a wonderful color and an inherent sense of motion. Here are several examples of a C major triad in first inversion:

When the fifth of a triad (e.g., the pitch G in a C major triad) is the lowest note, the triad is in second inversion. It's the least common position because it is very unstable — but that quality makes it perfectly suited to certain very specific uses when forward momentum is needed. It's also the position you'll hear as the last chord before a solo cadenza in most classical and baroque-era concertos. Here are examples of a C major triad in second inversion:

Knowing which inversion (if any) a triad is in is simply a matter of identifying which member of the triad (root, third, or fifth) is the lowest note. And figuring THIS out starts with identifying the root. A good site for practicing this is http://www.emusictheory.com/practice/chords.html.

High School Music Theory

If your high school offers a music theory course, by all means take it if you can. If it's offered as an Advanced Placement course, that's even better. You may even learn some counterpoint, harmony, and voice-leading, which form the core of college theory curriculum. But don't fool yourself — just because you took a high school music theory class doesn't mean you've become a ninja master.

All theory courses, especially those at the high school level, have to strike a balance between A) a user-friendly curriculum designed to ignite students' curiosity, and B) an uncompromising, pre-professional program in skill development. Great teachers make this balancing act look easy, but even they can't push you harder than you push yourself. In the end, just like in the performance arena, developing your theory skills is all up to you. The advantage with theory, however, is that you don't need a private teacher — just a computer with Internet connection. And of course desire, persistence, passion, a bit of obsession, curiosity, . . .

Coda

- ☑ Learn the names of pitches on the grand staff
- ☑ Learn to spell all major and minor scales
- ☑ Learn to identify and spell intervals
- ☑ Learn to spell and identify triads in all inversions
- ☑ Be able to do all of these spontaneously, without hesitation

CHAPTER 5 | Ear Training

Men trust their ears less than their eyes.

— HERODOTUS

Visual Society

We live in a sight-based world. Computers, books, television, movies, traffic signals, and even banners flown from the backs of airplanes reach us through our eyes. Cell phones were just for talking on, until they added high-resolution video touch screens — then they became "smart." And it's not just a matter of culture or technology: human beings are hard-wired for sight. In the brain itself, neurons devoted to visual processing number in the hundreds of millions and take up about 30 percent of the cortex, as compared with 8 percent for touch and just 3 percent for hearing.[17] But what's this got to do with music?

Too often we forget that the printed page of musical notation we read in ensembles or write in music theory class isn't "music" at all — it's only a visual symbol for what is essentially an auditory phenomenon. People don't go to concerts to look at sheet music. The music, after all, isn't on the page; it's in the air and in our ears and minds. Most languages have separate words for "music" as the auditory art and "music" as the printed page of notation (in German, for example, the

---

17 http://discovermagazine.com/1993/jun/thevisionthingma227

words are "musik" and "noten"), but in English we've become stuck with this one word that has to serve both uses.[18] It can cloud your thinking about what it means to study music, especially in music theory, and it leads to the next fundamental skill in preparing to be a music major.

When learning the fundamentals of music theory, simultaneously develop your ability to hear and sing scales, intervals, and triads. Become friendly with these musical building blocks in your ears, not just your eyes. Get to know them by sound as well as sight, just like you can recognize your friends' voices in the dark. The process by which this happens is called *audiation*.

Audiation

Audiation takes place when we "hear" and comprehend music for which the actual sound is not present, and it's the foundation of musicianship. It's the "inner hearing" that precedes thoughtful, accurate singing and playing. When we audiate, we're thinking in music, just like thinking in a foreign language. And just like learning another language, learning to audiate music happens in stages, over time, and only through frequent use. You can read more about audiation at http://giml.org/mlt/audiation.

Meet the Piano

One of the best ways to develop your inner hearing is to PRACTICE YOUR MUSIC THEORY FUNDAMENTALS AT THE KEYBOARD. The visual cues provided by the keyboard will help you immensely, and you'll also gain confidence in your budding piano skills. Less obviously but most importantly, your mind will build connections between the eyes, the ears, and the fingers. It's these connections which lead to musical "understanding." More about that in the next chapter . . .

---

18 You'll notice that throughout this book, I use the words "music" and "notation" to distinguish between the two ideas.

Hearing Tonic

The most fundamental ear/eye connection is to hear tonic as the most stable, restful, note of the scale. The best way to understand this is to experience it for yourself: sit at the piano and make up simple melodies in C major, using only the white keys. Try using mostly steps, but also use some leaps, repeat patterns on different starting notes, and mix it up however you like. It doesn't matter what it sounds like; no one's there to judge its artistic depth! What you SHOULD hear, however, is the natural gravitation back to tonic. Your musical lines just seem more satisfying when they end on the note C.

Tonic doesn't appear just at the ends of melodies, of course. See if you can identify which of the highlighted syllables are sung on tonic in the following familiar songs (answers below[19]):

1. **Hap**-py birth-day to you, hap-py birth-day to **you**; hap-py **birth**-day dear Rob- **ert**, hap-py birth-day to you.

2. **Mar**-y had a lit-tle lamb, lit-tle lamb, lit-tle **lamb**; Mar-y **had** a lit-tle lamb, its **fleece** was white as snow.

3. My coun-try **tis** of **thee**, sweet land of **li**-ber-ty, of **thee** I sing.

4. **Oh**-oh say can you see, by the dawn's ear-ly **light**, what so **proud**-ly we hailed, at the **twi**-light's last gleam-ing?

Singing Major Scales: Introducing Solfège

In the last chapter, you learned numbers ($\hat{1}$, $\hat{2}$, $\hat{3}$, etc.) and names (tonic, supertonic, mediant, etc.) for degrees of the major scale. Another system more suited to singing, known as Solfège (http://en.wikipedia.org/wiki/Solfège), happens to be the topic of the song "Do-Re-Mi" from *The Sound of Music*. Each syllable is sung on the pitch it names — making it a perfect introduction to this most valuable method. If you don't know the song, listen to it at http://www.youtube.com/watch?v=0m2RQWPfJ8Q.

19 1) you 2) had 3) thee 4) twi (And by the way, did you notice that the last word in each of these lines is also sung on tonic?)

Associating a particular syllable with a particular scale degree, regardless of which key you're in, is known as *movable-do Solfège*, and it's the system used in most college music departments in the US.[20] Musicians have used Solfège, almost unchanged, since the eleventh century; college music majors spend hours a week in its practice. Becoming familiar with it in high school will smooth your transition to college ear training. Start by singing major scales up and down, using Solfège syllables and checking your pitch at the piano. Pick a scale that's comfortable for your voice range and easy enough to play at the piano (I personally like C major).

After becoming comfortable with the scale, try simple patterns like these:

Make up your own simple exercises to sing, eventually becoming comfortable enough to improvise easy melodies using Solfège, just like you played at the piano earlier in this chapter. Feel and hear the natural gravitation back to *do*, and check your pitch frequently at the piano. You can also Solfège simple songs with or without reading the notation (http://www.8notes.com/traditional_sheet_music/), as long as you correctly establish where *do* (i.e., tonic) is. Remember, the first note of a song isn't always tonic; for example, "Mary Had a Little Lamb" starts on *Mi*.

---

20 The other approach to Solfège connects the syllables with pitches regardless of the key (C is always *do*, D is always *re*, etc.). It's known as *fixed-do Solfège*, for obvious reasons. This system is used much less frequently in the US, but is more common in Europe.

A Few Words about Singing

At this point, many instrumentalists get a little panicky about singing. If this is you, relax. Anxiety is natural when trying anything new, especially if you feel pressure to succeed. Instead of telling yourself, "I can't sing," say "I'm learning to be a better singer." Replace "I'm not a singer" with "I'm a musician who's becoming better at singing." Though your ego may tell you that your voice is somehow part of "who you are," try to see it as just another instrument to learn, with technique of its own like a violin or a trumpet.

There are more websites devoted to vocal technique than you can possibly view, and many are of questionable value[21]. As an instrumentalist myself, who has had to learn how to use my voice more effectively, let me boil it down to three basics:

1. Inhale deeply and low. Feel as if you are breathing into your belly.

2. Sing with a reasonably full, resonant sound, neither too softly nor too loudly.

3. Stay relaxed. Tension is your enemy, whether in the chest, shoulders, neck, jaw, or throat.

Solfège with a Drone

OK, back to scales. Eventually, you can give up the crutch of using the piano to check your pitch. Your ear will tell you if you're in tune, IF: 1) you go slowly enough and pay attention to each note, and 2) you sing with a drone that's sounding tonic (http://www.idrs.org/multimedia/midi/PUB/Drones.htm).

Start by singing the major scale to a tonic drone, using Solfège syllables and choosing a key that's in a comfortable middle range for your voice. Sing slowly up the scale and keep the drone sounding tonic the whole time; listen to your pitch and the drone simultaneously. Sing each note for a very long time and micro-adjust your pitch up and down, so that

---

21 Although far more detailed than you will probably need or want, the information and advice about the voice at http://www.voiceteacher.com/ is excellent.

you can hear what it sounds like to sing flat, sharp, and perfectly in tune on each scale degree. If you're sharp or flat, you'll hear beats of interference (kind of a "wa-wa-wa-wa-wa" sound) between your voice and the drone. The beats slow down as you sing closer in tune, and when you're perfectly in tune they stop altogether (http://en.wikipedia.org/wiki/Beat_(acoustics)). The easiest degrees on which to hear this are tonic, dominant, and subdominant, followed by mediant and submediant. It takes attentive practice (remember, nothing valuable is ever easy), but most people can learn to sing perfectly in tune using a drone.

Minor and Chromatic Scales

Solfège also incorporates all chromatic notes of the scale by changing the vowel sound on each syllable; a half step below *mi*, for example, becomes *me*. The following chart, adapted from http://en.wikipedia.org/wiki/Solfège, shows all chromatic alterations.

Major Scale Degree	Example in C Major	Solfège Syllable	Pronounced
1	C	*Do*	"doe"
Raised 1	C#	*Di*	"dee"
Lowered 2	Db	*Ra*	"rah"
2	D	*Re*	"ray"
Raised 2	D#	*Ri*	"ree"
Lowered 3	Eb	*Me*	"may"
3	E	*Mi*	"mee"
4	F	*Fa*	"fah"
Raised 4	F#	*Fi*	"fee"
Lowered 5	Gb	*Se*	"say"
5	G	*Sol*	"sole"
Raised 5	G#	*Si*	"see"
Lowered 6	Ab	*Le*	"lay"
6	A	*La*	"lah"
Raised 6	A#	*Li*	"lee"
Lowered 7	Bb	*Te*	"tay"
7	B	*Ti*	"tee"

Now you can Solfège minor scales, using the chromatic alterations to scale degrees where needed (this approach is known as do-based minor[22]). The three forms of the C minor scale, and their Solfège syllables, are shown below. Practice singing these at the piano, and then just with a tonic drone.

For a special challenge, sing a chromatic scale — first with help at the piano, then just with a tonic drone.

Singing and Recognizing Intervals

Continue connecting music theory fundamentals with your ears by singing the following interval exercises to a tonic drone. They're all written in the key of C, but you can (and should) sing them in a key that's in your comfortable range, and jump an octave down when it gets too high. Go slowly and check your pitch at the piano when necessary.

---

22 In yet another version of Solfège, the tonic of minor keys is sung to the syllable la. Predictably, this is known as la-based minor.

Another very popular approach to singing and recognizing intervals is to learn which songs outline specific intervals in their first two notes. Some music professors believe this method is very limited in value and discourage its use; others embrace it wholeheartedly. While the debate rages in music department faculty meetings, college music students keep using it. Personally, I'm all in favor of it, for this reason: if you can "hear" a song's first two notes in your inner ear and can sing them accurately, you're already audiating the interval. All you have to learn is the correct label (minor sixth, etc.). Practiced in combination with the Solfège interval exercise above, the following interval songs will develop your ears and build your confidence.

Interval	Ascending	Descending
Minor Second	Jaws Pink Panther	Joy to the World O Little Town of Bethlehem
Major Second	Frere Jacques Silent Night	Mary Had a Little Lamb Three Blind Mice
Minor Third	Axel F Brahms' Lullaby	Star Spangled Banner Hey Jude
Major Third	Oh, When the Saints Kum Ba Ya	Shoo Fly, Don't Bother Me Beethoven's Fifth
Perfect Fourth	Here Comes the Bride Harry Potter-Hedwig's theme	Oh Come All Ye Faithful I've Been Working on the Railroad
Tritone (Augmented Fourth/Diminished Fifth)	The Simpsons Maria (West Side Story)	Black Sabbath
Perfect Fifth	Twinkle Twinkle Star Wars	Flintstones Feelings
Minor Sixth	When Israel Was In Egypt's Land The Entertainer (large leap after pickups)	Love Story (where do I begin . . .)
Major Sixth	NBC "chimes" theme It Came Upon a Midnight Clear	Nobody Knows the Trouble I've Seen The Music of the Night (Phantom of the Opera)
Minor Seventh	Somewhere (West Side Story) Star Trek Theme (original)	An American in Paris
Major Seventh	Take On Me Superman	I Love You (Cole Porter)
Perfect Octave	Over the Rainbow When You Wish Upon a Star	Duracell commercial

A Few Words About Ear Training Software and Websites

There are plenty of good ear training websites where you can practice identifying and notating sounds played by the computer — intervals, scales, triads, melodies, rhythms, and even entire pieces. You should by all means take advantage of these free resources that didn't exist twenty years ago, and prepare yourself better than my generation did. Many college music programs even incorporate web-based ear training into their course requirements. An Internet search for "online ear training" will reveal dozens of useful (and some not-so-useful) websites.

Unlike theory websites, however, most online ear training sites can only evaluate "multiple-choice" type questions. In other words, websites can play something and ask you to label what it is, but the technology to actually listen to your singing and evaluate its accuracy is not widespread on the Internet[23]. For this, you have a couple choices. Ear training software can be purchased and installed on your computer, pad, or smart phone that can listen to your singing and evaluate your pitch. You can also do this the old fashioned way, by testing yourself at the piano. The next chapter will show you how the piano/keyboard can help you develop this, as well as many other aspects of musicianship.

Coda

- ☑ Play your theory fundamentals at the keyboard to connect eyes, ears, and fingers

- ☑ Learn to hear where tonic is in every melody

- ☑ Learn Solfège

- ☑ Solfège scales, intervals, and simple exercises and melodies with a tonic drone

- ☑ Utilize ear training websites and software, but also practice at the piano keyboard

---

23 One website which does "listen" and evaluate your singing pitch is http://trainer. thetamusic.com/.

Every single high school and private music teacher has been through ear training and sight singing classes in their college curriculum. Along with music theory, it's the most commonly required course for music majors. If you ask your teacher for some help with ear training, you'll be surprised how willing he/she will be to help. And like your instrument or voice, having someone help you REALLY makes a difference.

In the end, though, your success in ear training (like your success as a music major in general) depends on the quality and amount of effort YOU make. And your BEST tool to help yourself in theory and ear training is the piano/keyboard.

CHAPTER 6 | The Piano/Keyboard

*The piano is a universal instrument.
If you start there, learn your theory and
how to read, you can go on to any other
instrument.*

— EDDIE VAN HALEN

If a time-travelling scientist from 500 years in the future were looking through her time machine and saw that you wanted to be a music major, what gift of advanced technology would she bring to you? We'd all like to believe that the future will bring un-dreamt-of devices to aid in musical learning, but it's just as likely that she would just go to Wal-Mart and buy a $10 keyboard for you.

If you're serious about learning the fundamentals of music, there is nothing you can do to help yourself more than practicing the exercises in the previous two chapters at the piano or keyboard. For this, a ten-dollar kid's keyboard is perfectly fine. Of course, it's more fun playing a really nice electronic or acoustic piano — and if you're fortunate to ever play on a great concert grand piano, you will LOVE the sound! But if you or your family doesn't own a piano or keyboard already, ten dollars will get you what you need.

Special aside for pianists: of course I don't recommend you practice on a little electronic keyboard. On the contrary, if piano is your instrument, you should play on the best instrument you possibly can, as often as you can — either in your home, at school, church, a friend's home, or at your teacher's studio. It should have a standard size (88 key) keyboard with touch-sensitive, weighted keys.

Connecting the Eyes and the Ears

In my experience, one of the biggest mistakes that music majors make is that they don't take time to play and hear their music theory homework at the keyboard. They approach music theory as disconnected and abstract exercises on paper, rather than a way to understand what they hear in all music. Don't let this happen to you. Unfortunately, most college music programs contribute to this problem by separating music theory, ear training, and class piano into different classes, often with different instructors. Students who do their theory homework at the piano tend to make the connections between what they're doing in music theory and in ear training; they are the students who excel in all of these important classes.

Getting Started

If you're not a pianist, my advice is to just sit down at a keyboard EVERY DAY and play SOMETHING, even if it's just a C major scale. Its pattern of whole and half steps mentioned in Chapter 4 is very easy to see on the keyboard, where the half steps occur between E and F and between B and C. Don't play from notation at first — just mess around with scales, intervals, and triads. Pick out easy melodies by ear. Once you're relatively comfortable playing something with one hand, try playing it with the other hand. Also try playing it with your eyes closed to learn the "geography" of the keyboard in your fingers. To locate the white notes without looking, try to feel the groups of two or three black notes, and begin to memorize the feel of intervals. Also, when moving along the white keys, actually feel the "cracks" between the keys. Don't concern yourself with thoughts that you're doing it poorly or incorrectly, or that your technique isn't good, or anything else. Everyone has to begin as a beginner. Good pianists did too; they just didn't quit.

Hand Position

Keep your wrists flat and your fingers curved to reduce tension and avoid injury. There's a cute tip on piano hand position at http://www.teachpianotoday.com/2012/04/12/how-to-correct-hand-position-in-young-piano-students-its-qa-day/.

Eyes Up

When you're ready to begin reading notation at the keyboard, keep your eyes on the page, not your hands. It is SO tempting to look down at your hands, but it is SO limiting. If you tried to walk down a busy street staring at your feet, looking at each step, you'd constantly be running into people (and light poles, buildings, etc.). The keyboard is no different. Let your fingers learn the keyboard by feel, not by sight, and look at the notation on the page.

Keeping your eyes on the page shouldn't be a new idea. If you sing or play a wind instrument, you're already doing this all the time. Granted, on the trumpet there's no need to look at your hands to see if you're putting down the first or the second finger. Beginners on string instruments and guitar find it a little harder to resist looking at their instrument, and mallet percussionists face enormous challenges in this area. But try to approach reading music at the keyboard like driving a car: it's OK to glance down at the speedometer once in a while, but you'd better keep your eyes on the road.

You might be thinking, "OK, but how will I know if I'm hitting the right keys if I don't look at my hands?" Good for you! Excellent question; the answer is essential to developing musicianship: your ears need to tell you. Each time your eyes see a note on the page, your ears should hear it before your fingers play it; after each note, your ears should confirm or deny your fingers' accuracy by comparing the pitch they hear to the pitch they were expecting. Basically, your ears need to replace your eyes as the fingers' fact-checkers — but every time you look down at your hands, your ears are left out of this vital learning process. Keeping your eyes on the page trains your fingers, eyes, AND ears simultaneously. Powerful stuff.

Get Reading

If you need help learning the notes on the keyboard, http://www.emusictheory.com/practice/pianoKeys.html or http://www.musictheory.net/exercises are good places to begin. Start by reading notation that's relatively simple and that your ears already know, like scales, intervals, and triads, as well as easy songs. The examples in the previous two chapters are good to begin with because they're constructed of patterns that your ears can easily anticipate and monitor. Learn to associate the step movement on the staff (line to adjacent space or space to adjacent line) as step move-ment from one key to the next on the piano. Don't worry if putting two hands together (reading simultaneously from bass and treble clefs) doesn't come easily; it's much better to play with one hand than with none (i.e., not play the piano at all).

Playing Without Notation

When I was in high school, some of my most instructive times at the piano were playing without any printed notation, trying to copy music I heard on the radio or record player. You can learn a lot about music theory and sharpen your ears by trying to "figure out" rock, jazz, and popular tunes at the piano. Notate out as much as you can, too. A good way to begin is with the melody: its meter, rhythm, and pitches (and therefore what key it's in). Once you can play the mel-ody, try to play the bass in your left hand. Pretty soon you'll be filling in the harmony, too.

Coda

- ☑ Buy yourself an inexpensive keyboard

- ☑ Play some every day, both reading notation and just by ear

- ☑ Practice your ear training and theory at the keyboard

- ☑ Keep your eyes off the keys as much as you can, especially when reading notation

CHAPTER 7 | Rhythm

There are those who dance to the rhythm
that is played to them, those who only
dance to their own rhythm, and those who
don't dance at all.

— JOSE BERGAMIN

Here's a typical conversation between two college music professors about a freshman. Prof. X (band director): "Nick seems to be a pretty good musician." Prof Y (Nick's clarinet teacher): "Definitely. His rhythm is rock-solid. He can read anything."

We'd all like our teachers to talk about us in such a positive way, wouldn't we? Notice how the terms "good musician" and "solid rhythm" go together so well. Applied teachers expect their freshmen to develop a more mature tone through their college years, along with a larger repertoire, more technique, greater control at extreme dynamic ranges, a deeper sense of musical expression, and so on. But nothing is more impressive in a new student than secure rhythm. Be that student. **Develop a rock-solid sense of rhythm.** Paradoxically, to read music with perfect rhythm, you have to work a great deal WITHOUT music notation.

Get Physical

Rhythm is in the body, not in the eyes, ears, or mind. In hindsight, one of the best things I may have done for myself as a high school musician was to dance a lot. I was lucky to be at a large high school with a great dance teacher on the PE faculty. As juniors and seniors, we could pick what PE units we wanted to take; so along with scuba diving (I know, pretty cool . . .), I chose every dance class I could. Square dancing, jazz, tap, ballroom, and yes, disco too. I'm THAT old.

I'm not sure if my rhythm improved as a result of all that dancing or if I just gravitated to dancing because I had good rhythm, but even though I'm not dancing any more, I still want to. Music makes my body move, and I suppose my affinity for conducting has something to do with that. But that's just me; each person who feels rhythm in his/her body may express it differently. Pianists, string players, guitarists, and especially percussionists articulate musical thought very outwardly in their hands. It's harder to see in wind players and singers, but the fact remains: we produce music with our bodies, not our minds — and before you can master reading rhythmic notation, you have to develop rhythmic movement in your body.

"Put It On the One"

To me, this process begins with stillness, a complete ABSENCE of movement in the body. Well, except for breathing — keep doing that. In fact, tuning into the natural flow of your breath in and out of the body can help you become aware of that rhythm which already exists within you. It also has the effect of helping to quiet the mental chatter that interferes with concentration and focus. Find a comfortable seated or reclining position, allow your eyes to close, and just tune into the length and depth of your inhale and exhale without trying to change it or control it. You might also become aware of one other important natural rhythm in your body, the beating of your heart.

For the next few steps, you'll need to listen to one of your favorite recordings, something you know very well. It should have a moderate tempo and an absolutely steady pulse; most classical music does not work well for this. (My preferences run to Steely Dan or Journey, but jazz, hip-hop, funk, country, pop, etc. would be just as good.) Use ear buds or headphones, and try to listen to it without moving at all; just let the IMPULSE to move be the thing you pay attention to. By welcoming stillness into the body, it's actually easier to hear more.[24] Just keep listening without labeling, and rather than analyzing what you're hearing (e.g., "Is this in 2/4 or 6/8 time?"), let your awareness be on the duration between beats, paying attention to the fact that although some beats are stronger than others, the length never varies. If your breath can become synchronized in some comfortable way (e.g., in for four beats, out for four beats, or whatever feels natural), this can be a good way to begin connecting movement to music.

Next, firmly tap your dominant hand (right or left) on your thigh, the chair, a tabletop, or anything else — but NOT on every beat. Find the longest period that makes sense with the music you're listening to, tapping once every four beats, six beats, eight beats or more, perhaps connected to the rhythmic breathing you've been doing. Maybe it helps to think of tapping on the downbeat of every measure, or every other measure. The point is to move decisively and regularly but not too often. The more you move, the more you tend to pay attention to the movement, rather than to the internal impulse; tapping your foot on every beat (like you may have been taught when you were young) is actually counter-productive at this stage. Make sure your movement is exactly aligned with the internal impulse you feel in the music, and just stay with this for quite a while. This may be what the great soul and funk singer James Brown used to call "putting it on the one."[25]

---

24 If I'm having trouble hearing something in an ensemble I'm conducting, I'll make my beat pattern very small, to the point of not "conducting" at all. It's always amazing to realize how much more I can hear this way.

25 For an interview with Bootsy Collins, former bassist with James Brown, go to http://juicemagazine.com/home/2009/09/bootsy-collins/.

Two Hands are Better Than One

Eventually, get the non-dominant hand "hooked up" with the internal pulse by simply alternating hands on each tap, and observe what happens. Your non-dominant hand may feel a bit different, it might not align with the music's pulse quite as easily, it might hesitate or rush to the downbeat, it might be weaker or stronger, or it might just feel exactly the same as your dominant hand. Just observe — don't judge.

Gently turn off that critic we all have in our minds who tries to evaluate everything, and just watch, as though you were going to be called to a courtroom witness stand to report on what happened. Which fingers actually make contact with the tabletop? What is the relative weight in each hand? Where do you feel any tension or muscular effort in the wrists, forearms, and upper arms? What does each hand sound like when it strikes? Over time, you'll find your dominant hand "teaching" the other hand, and the two will feel increasingly equal. Once you're comfortable with alternating hands every measure or two, start tapping on every beat, first with one hand, then the other, then alternating.

Subdividing the Pulse

When tapping on the beat is comfortable and steady, add duple subdivisions, alternating hands all the time.

At some point, try substituting a metronome for the recording and play around with different tempos. Triple subdivisions are a bit more challenging; they have a natural lilt, or "swing," that alternates the beat from hand to hand.

Don't try to go faster than you can control; in other words, GO SLOWLY! Strive for accuracy, not speed. The goal is taking subdivision out of your mind and putting it where it belongs, in your body. **Constant subdivision of the pulse is one of the most valuable measures you can take to improve your sense of rhythm.**

Silent Pulse

Returning to your music player — if it has a "mute" button, try keeping the tempo going in one hand while you mute the music for a while, then un-mute the sound (a volume control works just as well). Are you still in perfect time with the music? Can you go four beats? Eight? Sixteen? Thirty-two? Feel the subdivision and the pulse simultaneously, and don't be discouraged; this skill, like all others, improves with practice. Being able to keep an absolutely steady tempo by just tapping it in your hand is a fundamental musical skill, and it's one you can easily practice whenever listening to music.

Egg Shaker

No, it's not a cooking gadget — I'm talking about those little percussion instruments you see next to the cash register at music stores. They're inexpensive, indestructible, and hideously annoying to others around you. With a little practice, you can become adept at keeping steady time in eighth or sixteenth notes to lots of music — practically anything with duple subdivision works. You can see a demonstration of some egg shaker techniques at http://www.youtube.com/watch?v=ADuFHwro4aU. Start with eighth notes, eventually progressing to sixteenth notes. For an extra challenge, try accenting the upbeats, or playing with your non-dominant hand.

Unfamiliar Music

Of course, you've got to be able to internalize the pulse and the sub-division in ALL music you listen to and play, not just music you're already acquainted with. Practice all of the above (listening in still-ness, tapping the pulse and subdivision, silent pulse, egg shaker, etc.) with music you've never heard before, in genres both familiar and unfamiliar. You can find all sorts of new music on Internet radio sites like http://www.iheart.com/, http://www.shoutcast.com/, and http://www.pandora.com/. The quicker you can rhythmically "lock in" when listening to something new, the quicker you'll be able to do it when reading and playing something new. And that's what sight-reading with good rhythm is all about, right?

Walking: Musical Rhythm Without the Music

Of course, not all rhythmic movement requires music. A very familiar practice of moving your body to a steady tempo, available to most everyone, is walking. We do it so much, it's easy take it for granted — but by paying attention to the quality of your movement while simply walking, you'll discover more of the internal rhythm that already exists in you.

What's revealing is not only the tempo in your feet — it's the quality of movements in the whole body. How large are your steps? Does your weight land on your heels or more evenly on the entire foot? How freely do your arms move? What does the acceleration and deceleration of your arms feel like as they swing? Does your head move when you walk, or is it relatively steady over your shoulders? What subdivision are you feeling? (It's also fun to observe other people's walking rhythms and imagine the music their bodies are making — you can get hooked on this form of people watching!)

Can you also observe the pace of your own breathing when you walk? What's the relationship between your breathing tempo and your walking tempo? Can you feel the tempo of your heartbeat, too? Very likely, you have some incredibly complex polyrhythms going on. For example, if you're walking at one hundred steps per minute (a moderate pace), breathing twelve times per minute, and your heart is beating at 120 times per minute, the rhythmic notation of that simple activity would be overwhelmingly difficult to "perform" — yet it takes place in each of us all the time, naturally and without thinking.

Beyond Steady Pulse

What's truly amazing about your natural body rhythms, however, is that they're synchronized with each other through CHANGES in tempo. If you run instead of walk, the rate of your breathing and heartbeat will obviously increase; but subtle changes in heart rate, breathing, and blood pressure also occur below our level of conscious awareness throughout the day, minute by minute. Similarly, so much music (especially "classical" music) mirrors this ebb and flow of body tempos in its own subtle changes in musical tempo.[26]

For example, listen to Arthur Rubinstein performing Chopin's Nocturne Op. 9 No. 1 in B-flat Minor at http://www.youtube.com/watch?v=7b3TNiPjQq4. This video allows you to watch the notation as you listen, so pay special attention to the evenness of the "steady" eighth notes in the bass clef. Not so steady, are they? Compare that to a perfectly accurate, but absolutely steady, MIDI recording of the same piece at http://www.youtube.com/watch?v=kjzkBbNdx0Y. Not musical at all, is it?

Used with good taste, these barely perceptible hesitations and surges of tempo help to communicate the music's structure and significance. Like great actors who imbue their lines with layers of meaning and subtext by changing the pacing of their delivery, sensitive musicians can bring out the tension and release in each musical phrase by being slightly flexible with the tempo. New avenues of musical expression are opened when your rhythmic control becomes this refined. Going beyond accuracy, great performances are also expressive — but if your rhythm isn't **accurate** to begin with, you CAN'T make the leap to **expressive**. That's why rock-solid, accurate rhythm is a fundamental skill.

---

26 Of course, not ALL music should be performed this way. There is beauty of another kind in music whose pulse is absolutely unvarying from beginning to end — from Renaissance dance music to jazz and rock — and whose effective performance depends largely on the performers staying in an absolutely steady "groove."

Reading with Rhythm

All of the preceding work should prepare you to read and perform music with a keener sense of internal rhythm. After all, when reading and performing music, you're re-creating what the composer created; but ironically, you can only re-create outwardly what already exists on the inside. Begin to see rhythmic notation as a representation of what essentially must come from within, rather than as a string of symbols that must only be "decoded." In other words, reading notation with solid rhythm is a three-step process:

1.   perceiving the written symbols and decoding them

2.   internalizing the written notation, making it your own

3.   performing outwardly what you have internalized

Step one is a cognitive process of recognition, understanding, comparison, and analysis; it happens in our minds. Step three is the physical process of creating sounds; it happens in our bodies. Step two is where the mind meets the body — and it's usually the most neglected step in learning to play with solid rhythm.

The Metronome

So at last, we come to the topic that's usually associated with improving rhythm — the metronome. This little torture device, this bane of our existence, is something you may already own but frequently neglect. FOR SHAME!! Use it every day, like your toothbrush. But use it wisely.

The most common use of the metronome is when you're working on technique and coordination with scales and articulation exercises. Beginning slowly and increasing the speed gradually is an excellent approach when your goal is rapid technique, but this is often the only way students use a metronome. Pushing ourselves to play faster and faster, we love to hate the metronome. It can start to feel like we're in a slave ship, rowing faster and faster to the beat of a drum (http://www.youtube.com/watch?v=WXh1tW16V-8).

A metronome, however, is nothing more than an external reference for measuring time; it cannot substitute for an internal pulse that is absent or unsteady. Remember, rhythm must originate where music is produced (in the body), so don't lean on the metronome like a crutch, letting its external "click" support you and carry you along. Instead, begin to see the metronome as the best way to calibrate and check the steadiness of your internal pulse, whether that pulse is fast OR slow.

Slow is Harder Than Fast

Slow tempos, rests, and long notes are challenging to keep in strict time, for the simple reason that the hands (tongue, lips, etc.) aren't actively articulating as much. The internal pulse and subdivision have to be stronger, because there's less external motion in the body. When evaluating someone's sight-reading at auditions, for example, it's always the longer notes — not the fast notes — which reveal the extent to which the performer has a solid sense of internal rhythm. The slower the pulse, the stronger the subdivisions must be felt.

The Slow Metronome

One of the most effective uses for the metronome is to MONITOR your internal pulse without DICTATING it. Do this by frequently taking the metronome down to half speed, clicking on every other beat, or even quarter speed, clicking on every fourth beat. (If you're in triple meter like ¾, click on every third beat, obviously.) Most metronomes don't go slow enough to do this; however, a simple and effective online metronome that does can be found at http://www.webmetronome.com/.

For example, if you want to practice something in 4/4 meter at quarter=120, set the metronome speed at 60 and feel the clicks as beats one and three;

even better, set the metronome at 30 and feel each click as beat one.

For a real challenge, set the metronome at 15 and try to keep your pulse steady for two full measures between each click.

Another way to test your inner pulse with the metronome is to feel the clicks as something OTHER than the strong beats. Start by setting the metronome to half speed as above, but feel the clicks as beats two and four.

This works particularly well for practicing jazz and rock music. A much greater challenge is to set the metronome at the quarter note tempo, but feel the clicks as upbeats, rather than downbeats.

Coda

- ☑ Try to read rhythmic patterns, not individual notes — much like you read words, not individual letters

- ☑ Fit these rhythmic patterns onto your steady internal pulse

- ☑ Feel the subdivision constantly

- ☑ Keep moving from downbeat to downbeat, even if you make a mistake

- ☑ Long notes are harder than short notes — don't rush!

- ☑ Rests are harder than notes — don't rush!

- ☑ Use a metronome every day

CHAPTER 8 | Essential Listening

Education is not preparation for life; education is life itself.

— JOHN DEWEY

You've been practicing fundamentals of ear training, piano, and rhythm. Your knowledge of music theory fundamentals is growing and becoming more automatic. You're practicing regularly. But where does preparing for a college music major actually involve "real" music? Right here.

If you're going to major in music, chances are you'll be studying Western classical art music. You know, music by dead white guys. **You should listen to LOTS of classical music to prepare for college music study**, because the more you know coming into your classes, the more you'll learn once you're there. The following list is a guide, or a place to start — and if you've already been listening to classical music, then here are some suggestions for how to continue.

You may not like all of these pieces, at least not right away, and that's OK. Most are relatively short, but others require prolonged attention. I've tried to present a cross-section of historical periods, and the twentieth century isn't neglected. The pieces are listed in chronological order, but feel free to skip around. I've also attempted to include music written for different performing forces: solo piano, solo voice with piano, chorus, orchestra, and so on.

DISCLAIMER #1: These may not be "the greatest" pieces of all time, but in my estimation they ARE pretty incredible. They aren't necessarily the most groundbreaking works in Western music history, or the most celebrated piece by each composer, either. What I hope they might be, however, is an engaging and inspiring preview to the types of music you'll most definitely hear, study, and perform as a college music major.

DISCLAIMER #2: Western classical art music DOES NOT retain the exclusive rights to "quality" and "artistic merit" in the musical universe; it's not the be-all and end-all of music. There are literally hundreds of musical traditions and styles around the world, and there's something to learn from great musicians in every culture. From a purely practical standpoint, however, classical music is mostly what you'll be studying as a music major, and most freshmen simply aren't as familiar with it as they ought to be.

RULE #1: When listening to vocal music, you simply HAVE to understand the text. Composers take great care in choosing which poetry to set to music, as well as how their music should enhance the feeling of the text. If it's in a foreign language, dozens of online resources have English translations of core vocal repertoire. Most of the videos of vocal music listed below have English subtitles for your convenience.

RULE #2: You don't need any special knowledge or background in musical analysis to do this. *Labeling* music (e.g., sonata-allegro form, etc.) isn't important until you have *experienced* music through lots of active listening. You only need two things: attention and memory. Pay attention as much as you can, and try to remember what you've heard.

RULE #3: And please don't think of this as an assignment, for heaven's sake — think of it as a gift of catch-up that you can give to yourself. It's just sensible to be familiar with some of the types of music your professors will expect you to come to know, appreciate, and value. Chances are you'll really like a lot of these pieces, too. And if you also experience moments of pure blissful transcendence, then welcome to heaven.

Exsultate Deo — Giovanni Pierluigi da Palestrina (1584)
LISTEN: http://www.youtube.com/watch?v=nRmkj19i4Yk
READ MORE: http://www.allmusic.com/composition/exsultate-deo-motet-for-5-voices-from-motets-book-v-mc0002358687

Palestrina served as the music director at St. Peter's Basilica in the late Renaissance, and he wrote almost all of his music for the Roman Catholic Church. With its flowing melodies, elaborate yet smooth counterpoint, and clear texture, Palestrina's music remains a model for musicians even today (i.e., freshman music theory). The text of "Exsultate Deo" is taken from the Book of Psalms: "Rejoice in God our helper: sing aloud to the God of Jacob. Take the psalm and bring hither the timbrel: the merry harp with the lute. Blow the trumpet in the new moon, even on our solemn feast day."

Goldberg Variations — Johann Sebastian Bach (1741)

LISTEN: http://www.youtube.com/watch?v=p7Nbx0Lv7zE
READ MORE: http://en.wikipedia.org/wiki/Goldberg_Variations

Sometimes cited as "the greatest" composer ever[27], Bach was known mostly as an organist and teacher in his lifetime, not as a composer. Thirty years after his death, Mozart discovered Bach's music and was greatly affected; fifty years after that, a public performance of his music generated even wider recognition. Influenced by the music of Palestrina written two hundred years earlier, and in turn inspiring composers to this day, Bach's music is the epitome of the Baroque style. The *Goldberg Variations* consists of a beautifully unpretentious aria and a set of 30 amazingly diverse variations.

---

27 http://www.nytimes.com/2011/01/23/arts/music/23composers.html?pagewanted=all&_r=0

"Hallelujah Chorus" from Messiah — George Frideric Handel (1741)
LISTEN: http://www.youtube.com/watch?v=C3TUWU_yg4s
READ MORE: http://en.wikipedia.org/wiki/Messiah_(Handel)

Like Bach, Handel was born in Germany in 1685; however, he was more widely acclaimed as a composer during his lifetime, most of which was spent in England. After a successful premiere in Dublin, *Messiah* gradually gained popularity to become one of the most frequently performed works in the classical repertoire. Originally written for a rather small orchestra and chorus with vocal soloists (as seen in the video link above), it became quite popular to enlarge the chorus and orchestra to huge proportions — in 1857, a London production featured an orchestra of 500 and a chorus of 2,000! More recent trends towards "historically informed" performance practice have attempted to present what scholars believe is closer to what Handel intended.

Eine kleine Nachtmusik — Wolfgang Amadeus Mozart (1787)
LISTEN: http://www.youtube.com/watch?v=rrZytaHypR4
READ MORE: http://en.wikipedia.org/wiki/Eine_kleine_Nachtmusik

You've probably heard the beginning of this piece a million times in commercials, elevators, and supermarkets — but have you listened to all four movements? The title in German means "a little serenade," though it's often translated literally (and incorrectly) as "a little night music." Mozart never intended to give it that name — it was just a little serenade in G major, probably commissioned by some wealthy nobleman for a party. In fact, Mozart's music has an uncanny way of presenting on two levels: if you're not really paying attention (if the piece were playing in the background at a party), you'd probably like it all right — but if you pay close attention, study the score a bit, and really listen to everything that's going on, you will be amazed at its depth and complexity.

Symphony No. 5 in C minor — Ludwig Van Beethoven (1808)
LISTEN: http://www.youtube.com/watch?v=KwNonij12tQ
READ MORE: http://en.wikipedia.org/wiki/Symphony_No._5_(Beethoven)

Of course you know the first four notes of popular culture's "go-to" piece of classical music. But have you experienced the whole symphony? The second movement is heartbreakingly beautiful. The third movement turns the four-note rhythm into a heroic and tortured dance that fades away and almost dies before your ears. But the transition to the fourth movement, where in a few measures death turns to joyous affirmation of life, is simply beyond words. There are some pieces of music that changed my life, and this one is at the top of the list. For a hilarious and insightful analysis of the first movement, listen to http://www.youtube.com/watch?v=f0vHpeUO5mw.

"Erlkönig" — Franz Schubert (1821)

LISTEN: http://www.youtube.com/watch?v=dc4ERZysvEg
READ MORE: http://en.wikipedia.org/wiki/Der_Erlkönig

Songs for solo voice and an accompanying instrument (guitar, keyboard) are among the oldest forms of musical expression, and Schubert's songs are absolute gems. "Erlkönig" tells the story of a father riding through the forest with his very sick son in his arms, while the son sings of his hallucinations of Death coming to take him away. Each character (Father, Son, Death) has his own theme (Death sings in a beguilingly sweet major key), and the son's repeated cries to his father rise higher and higher as Death comes closer and closer. I clearly remember hearing this piece for the first time in fourth grade (our general music teacher was brilliant), and it scared the hell out of me for years. It still does.

Prelude to Act I of Tristan und Isolde — Richard Wagner (1859)

LISTEN: http://www.youtube.com/watch?v=fktwPGCR7Yw
READ MORE: http://en.wikipedia.org/wiki/Tristan_und_Isolde

Richard Wagner was probably a pompous racist megalomaniac, but his music blasted a pathway out of the Classical era and into the modern one. "Larger than life" doesn't do justice to his conception of what opera should be, encompassing philosophy, mythology, religion, drama, poetry, and music—making it the perfect target for Bugs Bunny's comical satire in "What's Opera, Doc?" (http://www.youtube.com/watch?v=nI9Nbt7oJG0). In *Tristan*, Wagner transformed the ways that chord progressions moved, delaying the final arrivals so long and making such frequent use of chromatic scales, that a clear sense of tonic often becomes obscured. If you're OK with some ambiguity, you'll love this music.

A German Requiem, 1st movement — Johannes Brahms (1868)

LISTEN: http://www.youtube.com/watch?v=DGP7cBXpXqA
READ MORE: http://en.wikipedia.org/wiki/A_German_Requiem_(Brahms)

Unlike Wagner, Brahms extended, rather than transformed, the traditions of composers like Beethoven; he is often referred to as the most "Classical" of the Romantic composers. Departing from the Catholic requiem mass, which offers prayers for the soul of the deceased in prescribed Latin verse, and in keeping with his humanist views, Brahms himself selected passages for his requiem from the Bible that focus on comforting the survivors of the deceased. The first movement, for example, begins with the words "Blessed are they that mourn, for they shall be comforted."

Symphony No. 2, 1st movement — Gustav Mahler (1894)

LISTEN: http://www.youtube.com/watch?v=hZzFruQCofM
READ MORE: http://en.wikipedia.org/wiki/Symphony_No._2_(Mahler)

Known today as one of the most important symphonists to bridge the Romantic and modern periods, Mahler was renowned in his lifetime primarily as a conductor, leading orchestras and opera productions in Europe and New York. It has only been since the latter half of the Twentieth century that his symphonies and song cycles (he wrote no opera) have gained immense popularity with audiences and orchestras. His colorful and imaginative orchestration is matched by a firm command in creating large-scale forms; the entire Second Symphony lasts about an hour and a half. Themes develop slowly, but always with a sense of direction and forward motion. This is music that grabs you by the collar and makes you listen.

"Sì, mi chiamano Mimì" from *La bohème* — Giacomo Puccini (1896)

LISTEN: http://www.youtube.com/watch?v=IAwk14NuXjU
READ MORE: http://en.wikipedia.org/wiki/La_bohème

Confession: I know very little about the vast and magnificent world of opera. From its earliest forms in the late 1500's to the present day, thousands (maybe tens of thousands) of operas have been composed in every style imaginable. What I do know, however, is that Puccini wrote some of the most beautiful melodies I've ever heard; and if I were a singer, I'd want to sing them. Unlike the grand mythical settings of Wagner, Puccini's operas are romanticized portrayals of everyday people facing personal struggles and triumphs. *La bohème* tells the story of impoverished young artists living in Paris in the 1840's, and it was also the inspiration for the 1996 musical *RENT*.

"Clair de lune" from Suite Bergamasque — Claude Debussy (1905)

LISTEN: http://www.youtube.com/watch?v=-LXl4y6D-QI
READ MORE: http://en.wikipedia.org/wiki/Suite_bergamasque

Wagner stretched traditional rules of harmony to the breaking point; Debussy broke with them altogether. Curiously, though, Debussy sounds more familiar to our 21st century ears than Wagner does. Harmonic innovations such as parallel chords, unprepared shifts of key, and whole-tone scales have found their way into popular music and film scores; "Clair de lune" itself is featured in a memorable scene at the end of the 2001 movie *Ocean's Eleven*. The term "impressionist," originally used to describe the paintings of Monet, Renoir, and others, is sometimes applied to the music of Debussy and his contemporaries.

The Unanswered Question — Charles Ives (1906)

LISTEN: http://www.youtube.com/watch?v=tbArUJBRRJ0

READ MORE: http://en.wikipedia.org/wiki/The_Unanswered_Question

If there was an overall "style" of music in the Twentieth Century, it can only be described as a profusion of diverse styles. Rather than seeking to extend traditions and work within an established framework, most composers sought to invent unique and personal approaches to composition. Charles Ives had such a unique vision of music that he was virtually unknown as a composer during his creative years (i.e., no one thought his music was any good), though he earned a respectable living as an insurance salesman. As the first American composer to eventually gain worldwide renown, his music is still valued for its creative use of musical quotation, its eagerness to experiment with musical elements, and its ability to fuse disparate elements into a unified whole.

Petrushka — Igor Stravinsky (1911)

LISTEN: http://www.youtube.com/watch?v=JbWDG3LU4bc&list=PL1F88ABD9523A5181
(follow links to all four parts)

READ MORE: http://en.wikipedia.org/wiki/Petrushka_(ballet)

Colorful, dramatic, primal, rhythmic, incessant — these words are often used to describe the music of Stravinsky, one of the musical giants of the 20th century. *Petrushka* was one of three ballet scores composed early in his career that brought him worldwide acclaim (the others were *The Firebird* and *The Rite of Spring*). Each of these works draws heavily on folk tales and music from Stravinsky's native Russia. His free use of what most of us would call "dissonance" (listen to the trumpets at the very end of the ballet, for example) is somewhat tempered by Stravinsky's penchant for repeating musical figures and phrases: if you hear something enough, it starts to become familiar, then expected, then pleasing.

Six Little Piano Pieces, Op. 19 — Arnold Schoenberg (1911)

LISTEN: http://www.youtube.com/watch?v=bMoYrFjN52A
(follow links to all six movements)

READ MORE: http://en.wikipedia.org/wiki/Sechs_kleine_Klavierstücke

You have to listen a lot harder to hear repeated ideas in Schoenberg, who became famous (or infamous, depending on your point of view) for his AVOIDANCE of repetition. His early works continued down the path of harmonic ambiguity begun by Wagner, until all reference to a tonal center, or "key," was eliminated, such as in the *Six Little Piano Pieces*. Although he disliked the word, "atonal" describes his music quite well. Eventually Schoenberg devised a very strict, mathematical (some would say unmusical) method of organizing pitch wherein all twelve chromatic notes must be sounded before any can be repeated. Schoenberg influenced generations of composers in the 20th century, and tonal and atonal approaches to music have existed side by side ever since.

Ionisation — Edgard Varèse (1931)

LISTEN: http://www.youtube.com/watch?v=TStutMsLX2s

READ MORE: http://en.wikipedia.org/wiki/Ionisation_(Varèse)

If you've never heard of Edgard Varèse, you most definitely are not alone, but his impact on classical music in the 20th century was incredible. Instead of obsessing about pitch and tonality like Schoenberg, Varèse explored new possibilities of developing the musical elements of rhythm and timbre (tone color). He also was the first composer to embrace electronic music, and *Ionisation* was the first piece written for percussion ensemble. Frank Zappa cites Varèse as one of his strongest musical influences[28].

---

28 http://home.online.no/~corneliu/edgard_varese.htm

Concerto for Orchestra, 1st movement — Béla Bartók (1943)

LISTEN: http://www.youtube.com/watch?v=prwIYUAJhu4
READ MORE: http://en.wikipedia.org/wiki/Concerto_for_Orchestra_(Bartók)

Another singular approach to composition in the 20th century was forged by the Hungarian composer and pianist Béla Bartók. He became enthralled with his country's folk music, and he visited hundreds of Hungarian and Romanian villages, recording folk songs and dances on the latest technology, the Edison phonograph[29]. His harmonic language exhibits a highly individualistic fusion of folk scales with atonality, and irregular folk dance rhythms make their way into his music. But aside from all of that academic jargon, just experience the epic mystery and power in this piece.

Appalachian Spring — Aaron Copland (1944)

LISTEN: http://www.youtube.com/watch?v=CJYVH_kZkOk
READ MORE: http://en.wikipedia.org/wiki/Appalachian_Spring

Aaron Copland is perhaps the best-known American classical composer. Although he wrote music in many styles throughout his long life, he is primarily known for his "American" period of the 1930's and 1940's, when he consciously composed in an accessible, populist style. In its original form as a ballet score commissioned by the dancer Martha Graham, *Appalachian Spring* was written for a small orchestra of flute, clarinet, bassoon, piano, and strings. Like all of his music from this period, it somehow captures for me a spirit of optimism in the face of pain. The last section of the ballet is based on an old Shaker hymn tune, "Simple Gifts."

Le merle noir — Olivier Messiaen (1952)

LISTEN: http://www.youtube.com/watch?v=dCAMcaq1FB4
READ MORE: http://en.wikipedia.org/wiki/Olivier_Messiaen

Messiaen was an organist, composer, and ornithologist who lived and taught in Paris most of his life. His unique approach

29 http://www.flickr.com/photos/415384/5747480501/

to composition reflected a fascination with symmetry. Many of his rhythms are palindromes; that is, they read the same backwards and forwards. Pitch was also organized into scales based on symmetrical patterns of intervals, rather than major/minor or folksong scales. In spite of these seemingly artificial, intellectual constructs, Messiaen's music sincerely reflects his deep Catholic spirituality and his fascination with birdsong (*Le merle noir* translates as "the blackbird").

Le marteau sans maître — Pierre Boulez (1955)
LISTEN: http://www.youtube.com/watch?v=x2A30tJAH3s
READ MORE: http://en.wikipedia.org/wiki/Le_marteau_sans_maître

OK, so here it is: the piece of *avant-garde* music from your worst nightmare. Written almost sixty years ago, *Le marteau sans maître* ("the hammer without a master") still sounds freakishly random and unintelligible. This is the sort of music where people say things like, "My four-year old nephew could have written that." Paradoxically, and though it's nearly impossible to discern its language even after repeated listening, the underlying structures of pitch, rhythm, and other musical elements in *Le marteau* are complex and organized at an insane level. Setting surrealist poetry such as "On the dial of Imitation/The Pendulum throws its instinctive load of granite," this is atonality on steroids.

"Cool" from West Side Story — Leonard Bernstein (1957)
LISTEN: http://www.youtube.com/watch?v=xkdP02HKQGc
READ MORE: http://en.wikipedia.org/wiki/West_Side_Story

Leonard Bernstein was one of the most gifted musicians of the 20th century. He was a phenomenal (though rather showy) conductor, a prolific writer, and an inspiring teacher. As conductor of the New York Philharmonic, he hosted fourteen seasons of televised Young People's Concerts[30], bringing music education to American living rooms. His output as a composer, though

---

30 http://en.wikipedia.org/wiki/Young_People's_Concerts

uneven at times, is highlighted by some works of pure genius, like his score for *West Side Story*. A fusion of jazz, Latin, classical, and Broadway styles, it reveals Bernstein's appetite for musical diversity. The dance music in "Cool" is actually a fugue in the form of Bach, but in the style of big band jazz.

Short Ride in a Fast Machine — John Adams (1986)
LISTEN: http://www.youtube.com/watch?v=Pi4A9bPDvTc
READ MORE: http://en.wikipedia.org/wiki/Short_Ride_in_a_Fast_Machine

A lot of contemporary composers, like John Adams, have turned away from the severely atonal approach of Boulez to find their musical voice. Atonality, instead of being "the" way to music's future as Schoenberg envisioned, seems to have become "a" way forward, existing side by side with tonality in all its forms. *Short Ride* isn't so much about melody and harmony as it is about rhythm, color, and energy; a sort of Edgard Varèse meets Lady Gaga in an out-of-control Ferrari.

So there you go: twenty-one pieces of music. If you listen to only one of them a week, in less than six months you'll have given yourself a course in music history that you'll never forget. You'll also set yourself up to learn more in your college music history classes, because your professors' lectures will have something to "stick to" in your brain. Who knows? Your one true love, the music you've been waiting for your whole life, may be among the pieces listed here. Go listen!

CHAPTER 9 | Staying Motivated

Everything can be taken from a man but one thing: the last of human freedoms - to choose one's attitude in any given set of circumstances, to choose one's own way.

— VIKTOR E. FRANKL

Preparing for success as a college music major takes more than acquiring knowledge and skills. The most fundamental ingredient for success in any endeavor, by far, is that elusive quality called "attitude." It's really just how you choose to look at things, but it makes all the difference. **The most basic preparation for college music study is in your attitude, and in the realization that you can choose it.**

Things won't always go your way — you may not get in to your first-choice college, auditions might go poorly, you might not like some of your professors, you might struggle in classes, your roommate might snore loudly, and a hundred different challenges may present themselves. In fact, count on it. You can't always control life's circumstances, but when you realize that you're able to choose how to respond to them, you become responsible — spelled "response-able," or "able to choose your response." Becoming responsible is what going to college and growing into adulthood are all about, and one of the most powerful ways to deal with life's situations is to be proactive in visualizing what you want.

Seeing and Believing

As Steven Covey writes in *The Seven Habits of Highly Effective People*[31], every creation, from a beautifully controlled long tone to Beethoven's Ninth Symphony, is actually TWO creations: the inner creation that first happens in your imagination, and the outer one the world sees and hears, like a blueprint and a building. Without the first, the second would never materialize. Too often, though, we approach life passively, saying in effect, " I won't believe it until I see it with my own eyes." The creative person, on the other hand, says, "I won't see it with my own eyes until I believe it."

This is true whether you're trying to master a difficult passage on your instrument, finish a paper in music history, or nail your first job interview or audition. It's not just naïve "positive thinking" either. Good things won't happen to you if you just wish for them — you still have to work to make them happen. But seeing and hearing the desired outcome in vivid detail in your imagination unleashes energy, brings focus to your work, and serves as a self-check to keep you on course towards your goal. The same visualization methods that work for Olympic athletes can work for you, too.

Visualization

The goals you visualize should be detailed, multi-sensory, and infused with emotion. For example, let's say you want to nail your college audition solo. Create a video of it in your mind where you have the lead role, and also put yourself in the producer's chair. Who would you hire to record the sound track? Listen to lots of recordings by this artist. How would you describe their tone? Rhythm? Pitch accuracy? Articulation/diction? Dynamics? Expression?

Don't stop there — what would you be wearing in your video? How would you speak? How would you hold you instrument to look like a

31 http://en.wikipedia.org/wiki/The_Seven_Habits_of_Highly_Effective_People

seasoned and confident pro? What will the audition venue look like? How many people will be listening to you? What smells, if any, might you become aware of? Is there any taste in your mouth (coffee, perhaps)? Can you feel your alert but relaxed posture? What sensations would an outstanding performance create in the muscles of your hands, your arms, your chest, your throat and mouth, your embouchure? Noticing all these details of the "killer" performance, what emotions do you also want to become aware of? Now you're directing the star of your video — is he/she feeling poised or timid? Brash or humble? Secure? Cocky? Quiet? Loud? The more detail you can imagine, in all your senses and in touch with all your emotions, the greater your ability to stay motivated through the hours of practice that it takes to succeed.

If you ever have the chance to observe a figure skater preparing for his/her performance in the minutes before going onto the ice, notice the small movements they make in their legs, arms, head, and torso. They are literally going through their routine in their head and body, replaying their video and visualizing a perfect performance in great detail. The subconscious mind can't tell the difference between an actual performance and one in the head, if it's imagined with enough detail. Use this powerful technique for whatever goals you wish to accomplish, and you'll be amazed at the results.

Attitudes of Successful Music Majors

- ☑ **Curious** — The only way you'll ever learn anything is because you want to learn it, not because someone tries to teach it to you. Curiosity is what drives us to learn new things, and it's one of the qualities that makes us human.

- ☑ **Grateful** — Thanksgiving Day is nice, but one day a year just isn't enough. Taking your blessings for granted (your talent, teachers, parents, friends, music itself, etc.) is a sure way to annoy those around you and shortchange yourself, too.

- ☑ **Dissatisfied** — A balancing attitude to gratitude, dissatisfaction with the status quo can be a powerful motivating force.

The secret, if there is one, is to learn the difference between those things you can change (e.g., your knowledge of minor scales) and those you can't (e.g., who got the lead in the musical).

☑ **Compulsive** — Usually thought of as a negative trait, being compulsive in small doses might be OK. If you just can't go to sleep until you've practiced your etude, chances are you'll practice the etude.

☑ **Humble** — You're one of a kind, you're great, but you're not the center of any one else's universe. And we're all very small when you look at the mountains or the sea, or into a telescope. Be careful of your ego; it wants to be fed constantly. And remember, we learn from our failures, not our successes.

☑ **Self-Disciplined** — When tempted by the immediate gratification of TV, Facebook, parties, and other forms of "fun," successful music majors return to their self-made success video. Saying "yes" to your long-term goals sometimes means saying "no" to temptations.

☑ **Imaginative** — See above. If you can't dream it, you'll never achieve it.

☑ **Action-Oriented** — Balance DREAMING with DOING. As Thomas Edison famously said, "Genius is one percent inspiration and ninety-nine percent perspiration." All of the positive attitude in the world won't advance you one step toward your goals — you've got to work to make them real. Theodore Roosevelt, our 26th President and someone who balanced great ideas with courageous action, said, "Far better it is to dare mighty things, to win glorious triumphs even though checkered by failure, than to rank with those poor spirits who neither enjoy nor suffer much because they live in the gray twilight that knows neither victory nor defeat."

☑ **Persistent** — Keep going. Nothing valuable is ever easy; that's what makes it valuable. Calvin Coolidge, our 30th President, said it this way: "Nothing in this world can take the place of persistence. Talent will not; nothing is more common than unsuccessful people with talent. Genius will not; unrewarded genius is almost a proverb. Education will not; the world is full of educated failures. Persistence and determination alone are omnipotent."

Fundamentals

When I was in elementary school, an afternoon kid's TV show had a magic trick feature called "Trick and Treat." All you could see of the magician were his hands against a dark background. In two minutes, he would first do a magic trick, then he'd show you how it was done. Awesome. I loved Trick and Treat, but for some reason, what I really remember, to this day, is the corny jingle: "Here's Trick and Treat with the magic hands/We'll teach you how to do/The greatest tricks in magic land/The rest is up to you[32]." That's pretty profound for a kid's show. The rest IS up to you. The fundamental knowledge, skills, and attitudes for successfully entering college as a music major have been laid out in these pages, but they won't mean anything unless you apply yourself and practice them.

So we end where we began, focusing on fundamentals. They're the foundation and starting point for your college music education, and possibly your career. Every successful musician has worked to acquire them and works to keep them polished. Don't end your preparation for majoring in music here; don't put this book down and think you're done. You may know more ABOUT the fundamentals, but that's not the same as KNOWING the fundamentals. The rest is up to you.

> *If I am not for myself, who will be for me?*
> *But if I am only for myself, what then am I?*
> *And if not now, when?*
>
> — HILLEL

---

32 http://www.youtube.com/watch?v=NHARDEK4w6s&safe=active

About the Author

Robert Franzblau is Professor of Music and Director of Bands at Rhode Island College, conducting the Wind Ensemble and Chamber Winds and teaching courses in conducting and music education. Under his direction, the Rhode Island College Wind Ensemble has performed for the College Band Directors National Association and the Music Educators National Conference. In 2004 he founded the Music Institute at Rhode Island College for talented high school musicians. He earned the Bachelor of Music Degree from the University of Iowa, Master of Music Degree from Northwestern University studying conducting with John P. Paynter, and a Ph.D. from the University of Nebraska–Lincoln.

Rob is a contributing author of GIA Publications, *WASBE Journal* and *The Instrumentalist* magazine. He produced and moderated a series of live/online "Town Hall Meetings" on the future of music education and hosts the Rhode Island College Instrumental Conducting Symposium each January. In December 2008, he was named the third Music Director of the Rhode Island Wind Ensemble and has served as Assistant Conductor, Acting Artistic Director and Guest Conductor of the Boston-area Metropolitan Wind Symphony.

He is the founder/conductor of the Rhode Island Wind Orchestra, serves as past president of the New England College Band Association, is a board member of the Rhode Island Music Education Association and is active in CBDNA. Rob is a frequent guest conductor, clinician, and adjudicator throughout the country.